JENSONS JOURNEY

to Recovery

By Kimberley Shamtally

Jenson's Journey

RE-BIRTH AFTER BRAIN TUMOR DIAGNOSIS

It is a strange thing to comprehend that, in a blink of an eye, your normal everyday life can get turned completely upside down.

We were that typical family with a recent addition, born only three months earlier. Every birth has its story and Mason's was no different. He was tiny, the smallest out of our three children. He only weighed five pounds at birth but he had this distinct look of determination that he was going to be strong.

Mason arrived by emergency C-section due to my waters breaking early. He had run out of fluid and could not be carried until full term or he would be stillborn. As I had to comprehend this decision, it was my daughter's birthday and I just knew that he would be okay if he could hold on until the morning. After deciding to go home from the hospital to be with my children, I cried at the thought that he could actually die. At home, it was smiles and love for my son and daughter. It was her special day with Mum and Dad before our lives would change in the morning and the new arrival would be here. I couldn't sleep. Mason just had to make it and I needed to be strong. After saying good-bye to the children, Adam drove me to the hospital. The nerves were running high, but Mason had been moving, which was a good sign. After a tough night, he was born with the help of the amazing medical team, healthy but thirsty. As for me, I felt like my body had left the building. Recovery was going to take longer than last time and I needed to rest.

Feeling overwhelmed with the shock of how Mason arrived in the world, I cast my gaze over to my lovely son Jenson. He was two years old and every bit the typical toddler boy. Always running around, playing football, riding a balance bike, making friends and extremely good at understanding the world around him. I was proud of how he was developing into this bright, inquisitive yet calm personality. However, deep down, whilst I was lying in my hospital bed, holding my newborn son, my heart felt like there was something wrong. I was not sure what, but I just knew that Jenson was suffering. He would clutch his head and scream every now and then, then everything would be okay again. Being a more relaxed third-time Mother, I thought it was just a cold, a growing pain, a headache from all the noise...you know, one of the usual myriad of reasons why your toddler would cry.

However, three months later, I noticed that when he felt these head pains, as they were now, he would also become unsteady on his feet and have a tendency to fall over on one side. It was peculiar. I took him to the shoe shop to have his feet measured and I had his ears checked, in case it was a balance issue, but they were all fine. Every day when I would do the school run, I would secretly dread getting Jenson into the buggy or having to catch him and save him from falling, which seemed to happen every ten minutes. His big sister would help as much as she could. She even threw her own bag down to protect his head once when he fell. 'Why was this happening?', I would ask myself.

Then from the rush of panic and excitement of going back to school for my eldest Sophia, Jenson had his first day at pre-school. He had a great keyperson who would be looking after him on the days he attended. After settling in, I noticed that Jenson would pick up lots of toy cars and carry them around. They acted like a security blanket, protecting him from any harm. If I or the ladies at pre-school tried to take them away, he would have a massive meltdown and just cry. At home, he was much the same, only he'd lost his spark, and he no longer wanted to play outside anymore or play on his bike. The mere thought of it would make him sad and eventually he'd fall asleep.

His afternoon naps were something of which I was jealous. There I was feeding Mason every two hours and there was Jenson snoring his head off. He looked so peaceful. I felt bad when I had to wake him for the school run. Being new to pre-school, Jenson only attended the morning sessions, which meant that he was home in the afternoon. One day, when he woke from his nap, he came up to me and he was drooling at the side of his mouth. I had never seen him do this before, but I put it down to him having just woken up from a deep sleep. Even adults can do that.

Each observation that I noticed could be easily justified as nothing urgent, just more of the typical, everyday scenarios that all parents experience. It was only when I became more aware of a pattern that I had to investigate further.

Being a parent is like a full-time job, you are constantly monitoring every aspect of your child's life to ensure that they are healthy, happy and enjoying life. It was when I said those three words back to myself that I realised that Jenson was not experiencing any of these. As each day passed, Mason was growing stronger, as Jenson was becoming weaker. It was hard to watch him lose strength and not know what was causing it.

There was something going on and I needed some help from the healthcare professionals.

With all the love and support of my family reassuring me that there was nothing to be worried about and with his two-year review with the health visitor going well, was I just being overzealous about these traits? Intuitively, deep down, I knew there was something wrong, but how would this be taken seriously? There needed to be a reason to book an appointment with the doctor and there just did not seem to be enough information to go on, until one day at pre-school.

It was approaching half term when Jenson's keyperson noticed that his left eye had started to turn inwards and brought it to my attention. (I am extremely grateful for this observation as this would go on to save his life.)

I discussed going to the doctors to get this checked out as soon as possible, as this would surely have been causing the headaches and the unsteadiness. This could be the answer to Jenson's problems. It was the weekend, so I was unable to make a doctor's appointment straightaway, and this left me time to observe him and become confident that it was not something else. That weekend turned out to be the moment when I decided in my mind that Jenson needed urgent attention. He was so different to the little boy I used to know, he was getting worse and his problems needed to be investigated.

Monday turned out to be a regular day, the school run went okay, Jenson was feeling good although he did look pale. He was laughing at his little brother making noises, and he was helping me by fetching nappies and clothes. He seemed tired though and all the energy to run around had somehow left him. So, we agreed, that the next day I would put him in the twin buggy with Mason to take Sophia to school. As everyone rushed out the door, he was last and slower than usual. We approached the car and as Jenson stood up to hold on to the bumper while I put Mason into the car, he fell backwards, straight onto the concrete, with only his batman coat functioning as a cushion. I was shocked. This was bad news. My heart raced overtime as I picked him up and placed him in his car seat.

Jenson said, "I'm wobbly jelly, Mummy. Can you take me to see Dr. Ranj?"

Dr. Ranj is a CBeebies character on a BBC TV show that teaches children about various illnesses through puppets. It is set in a hospital, so that the children can understand why the character is ill and how Dr. Ranj will help him. Jenson really liked this show, it was one of his favourites.

I said, "Yes, Mummy is going to take you to see the doctor right now, although it might not be Dr. Ranj. Is that okay?"

"Alright, let's go soon. I don't feel very well," Jenson replied.

With that, I quickly got him and Mason into the car.

Jenson's Journey to Recovery

By Kimberley Shamtally

BOOKS BOOST BUSINESS

Books Boost Business is part of the Forever Family Forever Free group of companies whose address can be found at booksboostbusiness.com.

First Edition
First published in the UK 2022
www.booksboostbusiness.com
Book: Jensons Journey – Kimberley Shamtally
ISBN-13 978-1-913501-73-0

Table of Contents

For Jenson, the most amazingly determined boy I have ever known.

It is with thanks and deep gratitude for the support of my family and friends everywhere that I have been able to put this book together. They gave me the motivation on those bad days, and when I was feeling at my weakest point, they gave me the positive energy I needed to continue by carrying me and guiding me to the next stage in Jenson's recovery.

Thank you so much to the local hospitals and all the specialist neuro rehabilitation teams. The work that these people do is invaluable. It is one of the hardest roles to do, knowing just how much each child has been through, and yet they still manage to create a playful atmosphere to help them get their lives back. As a parent, it blew my mind just how much thoughtfulness and attention was given to each child, and how the relationships forged gave each child a love to be part of life again.

I would like to thank Jenson's rehabilitation team formed by The Children's Trust back in 2018 of physiotherapists, ophthalmologists, occupational therapists, speech and language therapists, dieticians, orthotics, play specialists, psychologists and GPs. A special thanks goes out to The Danny Green Fund, Riding for the Disabled, the awesome swimming coaches, my acupuncturist friend Jon, and special martial arts school Precision. These professionals have created the foundation for Jenson's recovery. However, if it were not for an excellent neuro surgical team, I would not be here telling his story today. Thank you, St. Georges Hospital in Tooting. I will always remember how you dealt with each problem the best way you could. As I mentioned to you, it was always going to be a team effort. And look at the size of the team – it just keeps getting bigger.

Surely with all the knowledge we gained, we just had to let people know what happens to a family when this type of diagnosis occurs. We all ride this journey together, picking Jenson up when he needs us.

Sebastian's Action Trust has been a recent addition to this growing rehabilitation team and is very much appreciated. Not least for the help it provides with Jenson but also for the help it can provide for the whole family. When you are a family in a crisis, this is by far the best support you be could offered. Not forgetting a special mention to Ronald McDonald House in Tooting. It was the charity that provided a shelter for my family. Located opposite the hospital, this place was a sanctuary. When we'd had a heavy day, the staff were there to listen and provide support. It offered a comfortable room within a much-needed family house, during times of treatment. It allowed us to gather our strength to continue each day, as our child battled with his life-threatening medical condition.

Friendships made along the way are like gold when you face the realities of the outside world. Each child at Ronald McDonald House has a different story, with their families under pressure but standing strong. We support one another as we know just how hard it can be. Thank you to each one of you, for your knowledge and experience, compassion and kindness.

Thank you for taking the time to make this a book of choice, to enable you and your child to become the best you can be both physically and emotionally after the diagnosis of a brain tumour.

We sometimes think the action we take to physically remove the tumor will be the end of our problems. But for a lot of families, this is only the beginning – as the child we once knew has now gone. We have a brand-new version. Our child looks like their usual self but has had a total reboot of all the information they have learnt over the years prior to their diagnosis. This is what we call "rebirth".

What happens now is that, as parents, we have a newborn baby again. The initial baseline of health appears good, but the assault on the brain will never really be revealed until much later in life. As a parent, this can be the news no one wants to hear or acknowledge. However, if we tackle this in a positive, proactive way, what we fear through the information given to us via a plethora of medical professionals may be diminished.

What if together we could re-train, re-teach and re-connect our children to the world they once lived in so that they can be the best versions of themselves? How do we find the right ways to get them eating, drinking, toileting and moving as others of their age? Where do you go for the right information? Is there a right way or wrong way to do this?

The answer quite simply is no. Always remember that each child's body and mind is unique, and will take as long as it takes to recover. All we can do is motivate, encourage and challenge what they know so that they keep learning.

Introducing **'Jenson's Journey to Recovery**

The aim of this book is to give parents of children with a brain tumour diagnosis some direction as to how to tackle everyday problems.

Surgeons are cool, calm and collected, the best at what they do, but they are not so good at telling you the consequences of your action to operate. Casually, they drop into the conversation that your child will need to re-learn everything, and because this is a life-or-death situation, you immediately sign that paperwork. It was only at this point that I found myself asking, 'What the hell have I done?' and 'What do they mean by re-learning everything?' Little did I know that it would be a complete memory wipe of the physical and emotional life of my child. Had I had known this, would I have changed anything? This is something every parent in this situation goes over repeatedly.

To put it simply, you had to act, there was no other choice apart from death. Once you get over this initial grief, you are then prepared to deal with what's right in front of you. This process of grief will be explained later and will hopefully give you the understanding that what you felt or are feeling is only natural, and not weak, pathetic or wrong.

Sometimes brain tumours can be easily resolved with early intervention. It all depends on the location, size, what type it is and if it is attached to any other parts of the surrounding area. Some children have multiple tumours, others have just one, but with all these situations, you still have the same problem. How do I give my child the best start in life after such a traumatic experience?

In my experience as a parent of a son with a low-grade pilocytic astrocytoma, it was hard to comprehend that this was my new life and one that included two other children – one older than him and one younger. One thing was clear, our family is a team and we needed to work together to get through this.

When you return home after the lengthy hospital stay, it finally hits you. Wow, how am I going to manage? What do I do first?

This book will help you to become aware of the healthcare professionals around you. Some of them are alternative practitioners, i.e. acupuncturists, massage therapists, osteopaths and nutritionists. The hospital therapist team will usually consist of speech and language therapists, physiotherapists, occupational therapists, ophthalmologists, orthotics, play specialists and teachers who all have specialist skills for neuro rehabilitation. These teachers have the patience and time to get to know your child through sensory play and to help them re-discover the skills that they still have knowledge of. They are absolutely wonderful people, they work tirelessly to ensure that your child will be able to go out into the world with the confidence that things will get better. What we must appreciate is that the time this takes to recover can never be prescribed, as every child is different and no individual prognosis will be the same as the last. So, with all the anomalies, we can only work on a personal level and only those who have been through the experience will know what works best for their child.

Through this book, I will explain how after brain surgery, my son later developed posterior fossa syndrome or cerebellar mutism as some might call it. This syndrome created a world of hidden difficulties and frustrations due to the lack of knowledge about it. As a parent, I had so many questions that needed answering and no one seemed to know the answers, which left me seeking information on anything and everything about this syndrome. I learnt that what we needed to do was re-connect the back of the brain to the front by creating a new set of neural pathways. The only way that could be achieved would be to teach instructions repetitively until the memory was instilled into the muscles and the neurons were created to carry information swiftly to and from the brain via the nervous system. Children have an incredible amount of neuroplasticity (the brain's ability to adapt), which with time can allow them to create new pathways to survive and thrive.

I am a complementary therapist by profession, but even with my 15 years of experience working with a variety of conditions, including with oncology patients, I still did not feel prepared enough for the work it would take to get my son moving again. It was as if all my training would be required on a 24-hour basis. This kind of rehab takes every bit of energy you possess. Sometimes you find that you need an outlet to vent your frustration or to re-charge. I started to look after myself by eating well, resting when I could and asking for all the help I could get. This is not just your battle, and you need a team to get you through. Allowing time for yourself means you are better equipped for the challenges that happen with your child. Do not feel guilty about this, you need to have a break and when someone offers to lend a hand, do not be quick to shut the door in their face. They can see what you cannot, otherwise they would not be offering their help. When you are tired, things can take longer than usual and because you are in this bubble, you can forget that you had a life before this traumatic experience. Friends, family, loved ones, counsellors and sometimes that stranger can provide you with the reassurance that you are doing the best you can. Believe it. As parents of a child with a brain injury, we are doing the best we can, and no one can understand this situation better than ourselves.

This book offers some points for you to consider on your own personal rehabilitation journey and highlights the areas that need your attention. You need to look at how your child's brain is recovering past information and connecting this to the new skills they are continuing to learn. This needs to be at a controlled pace, as we can often find that missing crucial physical milestones will only set them back later.

Nutrition is so important for the brain to get healthy and to be able to repair those areas that may have been damaged. Recently, a lot of research has linked gut health to the brain and how it affects the cognitive functions. Even if your child starts with a nasal gastric tube or a nasal jejunum tube, with the right guidance, they will be able to move on to eating real, wholesome food. Think of the weaning stages of a baby. Your child will be able to move from liquids to solid food, but at a slower pace than before due to the lack of muscle tone needed to actively breakdown food. Time is a great healer and with all the medication that your child may still be on or has taken in the past, their digestive system will need time to heal and repair. Your child may find it difficult to tolerate real food in the initial stages of treatment and recovery, but it does get easier as they gain more strength.

Finally, it is worth remembering why you chose this book. It was to find answers to certain types of problems you may be experiencing post operatively. If your child is due to start nursery, pre-school, primary school or college, they will need a good team of therapists around them. As a parent, this book will give you confidence that you can also help by observing what works and what does not work for your child. If your child does not have their voice back, you will be their way of communicating with everyone around them. Just think of all those hours we spend watching our children. We can see subtle differences that other professionals cannot. Learning is not just through the dry methods of recalling facts and looking at pictures. We have all the other senses to consider. This book will help you be more open to other ways of processing information, so that your child has more chance of recovering most of the skills they used to know. Never forget the wonderful world of neuroplasticity and how children are the most resilient beings. They are always ready to learn something new, we just need to show them how.

Part I:
Discovering the Tumour (Dealing with the Diagnosis)

"From a place of unimaginable pain, life goes on. What now? What will happen? The ground opens and you feel like you're falling, falling uncontrollably, overwhelmed with complete darkness, the life you knew suddenly shattered into a million pieces. What do you do first? No one can ever imagine what you are truly going through. It is with utter disbelief, guilt and sadness that such a terrible tragedy could happen to a beautiful child. Time seems to stop, nothing else matters. Time becomes a way to heal those hurts, to deal with grief and allow hope into your heart. With hope, a chance of life, one that will be spared and take on a new direction. "Never give up, never give in. Look inside yourself, to find the strength within."

Kim Shamtally

Chapter 1:Tumour
(A Need for Medical Intervention)

Jenson

When Jenson came into the world, he was one of the quietest babies. He did cry, but it wasn't anything that I couldn't handle compared to my daughter who would scream until the midwife would enter the room and swaddle her with a soft blanket. I just thought, "Wow, what a pleasure." He had these large dreamy eyes, the colour of sand, like his Dad's. He was beautiful and acutely aware of my presence.

It's an intense moment, when you realise you love your baby. It's just a different bond, it's soulful. I can't explain it. With Jenson it was like a rush of bubbles, a warm affectionate bond, instantaneous. I was already in love with him from the first moment. That doesn't always happen when you have children. It can take a while as you recover from the birthing experience. I just swaddled him and cuddled him a lot, making sure he was alright. At night he would feed and sleep before all the other babies woke up. He was in hospital with me for a couple of days, because I had to have an emergency C-section after my waters broke but the contractions failed to progress. I had bounced on that birthing ball and walked up and down stairs all day. Nothing was happening. So into theatre we went. As smooth as the delivery may have been, my anaesthetic wore off too soon. I could feel every tug, pull and rummage around my abdomen. In the end they had to put me under general anaesthetic as eight more minutes of the procedure were left and I could not last that long in serious pain.Jenson was born healthy, with no cause for concern. We were just so excited to meet him as he was over a week late and showed no signs of making an appearance. We managed to leave the hospital on the third day and go home. Family life felt complete.

My daughter accepted Jenson just fine. She was the big sister telling him what to do, even though they couldn't really talk to each other. She was like, "I'm going to look after you." She enjoyed bringing toys and nappies for him, and as he grew, she developed a strong bond with him. She wanted to do everything with him and he wasn't hanging about with his progress. He was keen to take on the world and it was just amazing to see the little progressions he was making with his movement, sitting up, toddling along with his walker and drawing his favourite Paw Patrol characters. It really startled me that he got the hang of this whole walking thing very quickly, and how he was soon playing football, dribbling the ball between cones with his friends.

If I was dropping off my daughter to school, he'd be playing with some of the reception kids and they'd be kicking the ball to him and he'd be joining in, and I'd think, "How amazing." And he was getting tall. Our family is not particularly tall. I'm 5'3". So, if he was going to be tall, that was going to be coming from his Dad's side.

One of the parents from my daughter's class said, "Wow, how old is he?"

When I said, "Oh, he's 18 months", she replied, "He's looking good, isn't he? He's tall. He's big for 18 months."

I didn't take any notice of her comment. I just thought, "Yes, he gets it from his Dad's side, his Grandad is 6 foot, so that'll be okay."

I started thinking, "Maybe he's going to be a footballer." Then he started learning to ride his balance bike. So, then I thought he was going to be into biking. He seemed to be outdoors all the time, he didn't want to be indoors. He was always outside, always in shorts, he didn't like trousers, and he was easy-going. Even with food, nothing was an issue, he would try anything.

Then, it got to a point where we realised that actually there are certain things that he can't tolerate, like orange juice and ketchup, which became his food sensitivities, but he still tried to eat and drink them. I think one of his best qualities, even now, is that he has that ability to just tackle anything. If you give him something new, he will try it, and that hasn't changed one bit.

As he got to twenty four months he was trying to walk, I did think, "Oh, he's a little bit wobbly", but most children are when they're trying to get their balance and co-ordination, so I didn't think anything of that at all.

He was toddling along, getting faster with it as well, because everything has to be quick with Jenson. We didn't name him after the racing driver, it was purely because we thought, "He looks like a Jenson, very cheeky." His general milestones had been met, nobody had any suspicions about his progress. The health visitor had no reservations, the doctors were all happy with him, everyone was happy with him. In the general red book, it said nothing remarkable. (These red books are given to every parent of a newborn child in the UK, to record information about their health and data with regards to height, weight and head measurements.) That's what they said, "unremarkable". So, in other words, he's fine, and they didn't pick up on anything in particular. It was really a matter of "did we have anything that was concerning *us*?"

One thing I did notice just after his second birthday was that he had grasped the idea of jumping, but he couldn't actually jump, and I thought that was odd, as children are normally jumping through furniture or doing something crazy on the trampolines at their pre-school and nursery clubs. I didn't see him do that, but I just thought, maybe that's not his thing. It did sit in my mind though. Although he started walking early, he didn't walk securely.

If Jenson was having a wobbly day, I'd just pin it down to tiredness and I'd put him in the buggy. I noticed that I was getting incredibly tired and feeling hungry, bit sick with some dizziness. Oh my God, a quick mental check of my monthly cycle and a dash to the nearest pharmacy. Congratulations you are pregnant, again. How will this work? The babies would be too close together. A nervous phone call to Adam, turned out to be a celebration, he was delighted. I had to do the school run every morning. So, it was always a bit, go, go, go. Adam was at work all the time, and I was heavily pregnant with Mason, so I just had to get on with things. Jenson seemed to nod off most afternoons, he would have a little afternoon siesta, but he was growing, so we just let him. I didn't think much of the naps, as most children around his age would do this.

It's not until you piece these observations together that they make any picture that suggests something more serious. I thought, "Yes, the balance thing, he is just not getting it. And the jumping thing's a little bit of a worry", but I was still two months away from having Mason. I had to go into hospital for regular checks due to my previous surgeries. At this point all the attention went to my impending birth of my third child.

Mason

My daughter's birthday is in July, and Mason was due at the end of July. My waters broke, so we had to go in to have a scan and make sure everything was okay. The scan showed that Mason was in distress as I had lost a lot of amniotic fluid. They said, "If we don't deliver him the next day, he's not going to make it, he's going to be stillborn. He's not going to go full term."

Obviously, I was very distraught because I thought, "How could I have missed that?" I didn't even realise, the movements were so low down and he'd got into a bit of trouble.

When they said that he was going to be stillborn if we didn't do anything about it that day, I just burst into tears. I needed to be at home with my daughter because it was her birthday and they were saying, "You are absolutely crazy. What are you doing? We want to keep you in hospital to observe you so that you can be ready for surgery."

I said, "I can't do this now. I'm going to have to really trust myself here and have faith in the fact that Mason will be good for tonight so that I can spend some time with my daughter and celebrate her birthday. I'll be back in the morning."

They said, "You'll be back here at six o'clock in the morning, because that is the latest we will expect you."

I said, "Yes, okay, but I'm not staying here tonight."

They were shocked because all they obviously wanted to do was to make sure the baby was well and that neither one of us were in jeopardy. But I had to be true to the situation. I couldn't miss my daughter's birthday. I wanted to prepare her for the new arrival and make this transition as beautiful as it could be. My daughter was a worrier and my closest friends were on watch to make sure she understood that I was going to be okay, but I would need to stay at the hospital for a couple of days.

So, I went home and that night was very scary because I had to be aware of Mason and just make sure he was still doing some movements, and there was a real prospect of, "God, what if he is going to die? We're never going to meet him."

But I put it to one side, because I'd made the decision to spend that time with my daughter, because I knew I was going to be in a situation for the next few days where I didn't know where I was going to be emotionally, and I just wanted to be happy for her.

She had a lovely time, she got an awesome iPad, spent some time with Nanny, and she was happy enough. Jenson, well, despite the way the attention had all gone to Mason, Jenson was the best little boy ever. When you wanted to be somewhere you needed to go, he always understood. He understood if it was important, he understood if you had to leave him with Nan and Grandad. He was okay with it, he never kicked up a fuss with us. But every now and then, he'd have a little bit of a headache and he'd get upset about it. We'd just look at him and go, "What's that all about?" But there was just so much going on, and we thought, "Well, we'll sort that out as soon as we can." And, he would be like, "Okay Mum, okay, Mummy, I'll see you later."

He was just an absolute delight, and I didn't want to leave him behind to go to hospital because I knew I'd have to stay in there. I don't like leaving my kids. So, as I went into hospital, they were really giving me a hard time because of all of the things that could have happened, but in the end, Mason was fine. His heartbeat was strong and he wasn't in any distress. I wanted to have him naturally, without pain relief, and they tried to get the contractions going. Unfortunately, they didn't progress, so I had to have an emergency C-section.

It was touch and go. He was so, so small, the size of my forearm, that I thought I'd break him when I held him. I was distraught that we'd nearly lost him. That shock stayed with me for such a long time. The hospital experience was not what I anticipated. You're supposed to be happy after the birth and have these balloons that say, "Congratulations. You're parents again, a lovely little boy." We were like, "Oh thank God. We've got our little boy. He was in there and he was starving." And the first thing he wanted was a drink, cue the breast milk. For this, I needed to put myself into a calm space, as the milk would be hard to create. Luckily, Mum was abundant and Mason was settling into life on the outside. Devilishly handsome, his eyes were huge and soul searching. He was safe, I was safe, we both made it through the surgery.

So, with all of the surgeries I had experienced – because all my kids had come out through the sunroof – it floored me physically, and took me a week to come round and recover from it. It was tough because being the third pregnancy, my body was taking that much longer to get going. All the hospital staff were trying hard to get me up and about, but I think in the end, it was through my sheer frustration and anger that they couldn't bring Mason to me quick enough when he was crying that made me stand up and go to him and pick him up. Before then, I was hunched over in pain and collapsed. My stitches were sore, particularly on the right side.

Then the nurses were all like, "Wow, look at you. You're determined to go home. Aren't you?"

I said, "Yes. Get me out of here. I don't want to be in the hospital."

So, with that, I had another two days in hospital while they observed me, and then we went home. It was an ordeal that I was relieved to get through.

Mason was tiny. My Mum was worried sick when she came around to see him. I actually asked her to come around because I needed reassurance, I suppose. It's at these times that you connect with your mum the most. That is, when you have children yourself.

She just looked at him and said, "Oh, he reminds me of you when I had you, and you were premature and so tiny, but he's going to be great, he's going to be fine." She had a remarkable way of comforting me.

Mum was amazing like that. She would come around with her little bag with treats for the kids. She always used to treat them fairly. If one got a present then they all did. She was so good like that, little toys, baby grows, too many magazines. They would just stack up to the roof.

She'd go, "Oh well, I know you've got more than enough. He will grow into them."

She'd always pick Mason up and just get cracking. I never had to tell her anything when she'd come over, Mum was just hands-on, she loved it. It was very good for me so I could recover. My body felt like it had been turned inside out. There is nothing easy about having major surgery, especially when you have other kids to look after and a partner who worked full-time. Mum wanted to be involved. She was always checking in. If she didn't come over, she'd be calling to make sure that Mason was all right. She always used to keep an eye on Jenson too. She was fiercely protective.

Mum was never overwhelming. She didn't do the overbearing parent. You see it so many times when you feel like you've got another person in the room trying to parent on your behalf. She wasn't that kind of parent, she allowed me to do my thing, but was always there to support me. If anything was up, she'd be like, "That'll be okay. Just give him time."

It was reassuring and calming, because you never realise quite how stressed you're getting or anxious you're getting about absolutely nothing, and it's just that hand of reassurance on your back going, "It'll be fine. Do you want a cup of tea? Maybe, have something to eat." Always something to eat. She used to say that all the time. "Sit down, have a rest, put your feet up." And would I take any notice of her? No, I never did. That's where we were different, but she was very good at highlighting the need for rest and space and peace and quiet, which I never valued until recently.

Jenson, obviously, was seeing a lot of her and she was always saying how great he was as a little boy. She really enjoyed being with him and he was becoming a bit of a musician. He liked playing the toy piano and she was teaching him a lot of things, and he was learning his colours. She'd say, "He's so smart. He's really, really clever. I'm so proud of him." In those moments, I would just be calm, and know that we'd actually come through and we were going to be okay.

Obviously, Mason, gave us a few frights, because of him being so small. We had a brief hospital stay due to suspected meningitis but we knew that he would be okay. The doctors mentioned how brave he was, even though we never got to know what was causing his breathing issues. Mason decided "That's it. I'm here now. I'm just going to appreciate that I'm outside and learning about the world around me."

Something's not right

I realised one day that Jenson was particularly unwell. He'd had an afternoon nap and as he'd got up, he just had this little bit of drool round his mouth, which he hadn't had before. He just looked pale, not himself, you know, really sad.

I asked him, "Are you okay, Jenson?"

He said, "Yes, I'm just a bit tired, Mummy, but okay."

It was when he started preschool that they noticed something. He'd only been there a month, when they said that his left eye had started to turn in. I thought, "I haven't seen that before."

They said, "He was playing with his toys, his cars, and then he was at the table and then his eyes started turning inward."

That was definitely not a good sign. My whole internal dialogue and my body were thinking, "Prepare for something. That's not adding up, just not making sense."

The nursey said. " He was playing with his toy cars at the table, and then we noticed that Jenson's left eye started to turn inward."

"Jenson's key worker Karen said, " Do you think you could get a doctor's appointment?"

I said, "Yes, sure. I need to get a doctor appointment for Mason, so I'll book Jenson in also."

"Yes, do that over the half term," urged the teacher.

A couple of days later, Jenson fell over. We were getting ready to take Sophia to school in the car. Jenson was holding on to the bumper and then just fell backwards, without looking for support at all, he just fell backwards. He had this Batman coat on with the little ears a padded, winter, coat, and it was quite snug, which was lucky because it protected his head as he hit the concrete. Alarms were ringing in my head. You could see him falling, but it was so fast, that I could not catch his hand or break the fall. As I sat Jenson up, he was white as a sheet. I said, "Just wait there, I'll just go put Mason in the car."

A cold sweat came over me. I was hyper, driving in such a panic because I thought, this is terrible, what's happened to him? I've got to get him to hospital, but what am I going to do? I've got Mason with me and I've got to take Sophia to school, and Adam's at work.

"Mummy, my mind is just going overtime." I got him in the car, and he said, "I feel like wobbly jelly, Mummy. I don't feel very well, I need to see the doctor."

I told him, "Yes, definitely. We're going to go. It might not be with Dr. Ranj", because he was obsessed with Dr. Ranj. "Is that okay?"

He said, "Yes, yes, Mummy, I'm fine. That's fine. I'm very wobbly, I feel like jelly." He just kept saying jelly all the time.

There was a BBC TV CBeebies character, I think it was Mr. Tumble, who said, "jelly on a plate", and I just kept feeling like jelly, almost seasick, like everything was bobbling around me because I didn't know what to do first. So, I just got in the car, dropped Sophia off to school and then went straight to my Mum's to see if she could take Mason, so I could take Jenson to A&E. But it didn't work out that way, because she had to be at the doctor's surgery herself. She was apologetic that she couldn't be there. At the same time, she said, "Oh, it'll be fine. Don't panic. It'll be fine, but just be calm."

I thought, "No, no, no, this is the wrong response. No, no, this is not the time to be calm. I've got to go."

She said, "Well, don't just go off like that, give them a call."

It was so difficult to get hold of anybody to get a GP appointment, and even after explaining the urgency of my son's condition, they were saying, "There's a two-week wait, that's the soonest we can do."

That was just not good enough. Being a new mum again, I was in that highly emotional state. I complained, "What do you mean two weeks?" Then in an aggressive outburst, I said, "This is not good enough."

I had to push them for another way to get Jenson seen. The receptionist mentioned the Walk-in Centre and the '111' Service.

NHS or National Health Service 111 is the free number to call when you have an urgent healthcare need. It directs you to the right local service, first time. It is available across the whole of England making it easier for you to access urgent healthcare services when you need medical help fast. It is available 24 hours a day, 365 days a year.

Taking a few deep breaths, and with my hands shaking, I called the emergency 111 service. It was very scary making that phone call as I had no clue what was wrong with my child, but I told them all the symptoms. So, that was me really reliving in my mind's eye all the images of him and what I'd seen. I had to tell them very clearly about the things that didn't seem right with Jenson. I think it is so important to be clear and provide as much information as possible, because that's how you know you're going to get the right attention for the diagnosis and the right investigations, by recalling the facts, but because as I was recalling the images, my mind was bringing up other memories, "Oh, yes, he couldn't jump. Oh, his eye was turning inward. He had wobbliness, unsteadiness. He sometimes seemed to be holding his head, he had short, sharp headaches."

I just reeled it off a whole string of symptoms, which they took seriously. I honestly think it's the way you deliver it as well, that makes them that decision.

They were particularly good at taking down my concerns and, as if by luck, I spoke to a man who was particularly thorough and checked everything I said with his manager. With that, the advice was to take Jenson straight to hospital.

I can't thank them enough, because when you were looking at Jenson, he was okay, you couldn't see anything. You'd just think, "Oh, he's having an off day." So I took him to A&E. As my Mum couldn't be available, I was in a terrible mood. I just thought, "I need to get out of here."

When you are in that zone of stress, you find some extra strength you don't realise you have. So, I picked Mason up in his little carry cot and he was heavy, it felt like I was picking up 10 kilos, and I stomped out of my Mum's house in silence, whilst closely watching Jenson walk rather unsteadily towards the car. My body had no time to complain about the pain of my C-section scar as I got down to the hospital quick sharp.

My Mum was like, "Hold on a minute, maybe I can change..."

But before she could finish, I said, "Well, don't worry about it. I'm doing this by myself."

So, I got there. I was actually shaking. I remember driving the car shaking. I was just so worried about Jenson. He was quiet too, but at the same time, I think he was relieved that I was acknowledging it, whatever it was, because we didn't have clue what it was.

So, when I got to the car park, I couldn't get through the gate. My brain was just not thinking properly. I just needed to press the button for a ticket.

But I kept chanting, "So, why don't you bloody open? What's wrong with you?" Then I pressed for assistance.

The guy was like, "Have you pressed the ticket button?"

I shouted, "Of course, I've pressed for a ticket. I've been coming here for ages. I just had my son here."

He goes, "Could you press it again for me?" He was the calmest person ever. "Please press it again." Of course, the ticket appeared.

"Oh, thank you."

I was so short with him. I don't know where my mind went, but I got there. I parked very badly because I was just in a different realm of stress and I got hold of Jenson. I was trying to keep hold of him because he kept falling over, but I just had to get him into the hospital. In hospital car parks, nobody parks that well. And this BMW 4x4 decided to park next to me and gave me zero space to get my kids out. Boy, did they get it when they got out of the car.

I was just like, "Right, how am I supposed to get my kids out of the car? I need to get to the A&E department urgently."

The man was that flustered.

I said, "If you could just move your car..."

He said, "I was just going to suggest that, if you'd give me a minute."

He moved his car and I got the twin buggy out. That's when he helped me. At that moment in time, it was just like a whirlwind. I accepted his help and I thought, "Thank you." But I didn't have time to sit and appreciate it. I just had to get Jenson inside. It felt like an eternity, waiting around, just knowing that there was something terribly wrong with Jenson.

Diagnosis

When we arrived at hospital reception, we were met by the Children's Accident and Emergency team. The doctors were concerned about the way Jenson was so wobbly and weak down his left side. Immediately, they made notes of his recent headaches, left eye turning inwards and falling over. The usual observations were made, height, weight and pupil response, blood pressure, temperature, and pulse.

Everyone in the hospital was very attentive. I couldn't fault them for taking my concern seriously. I think that is the big difference between being acknowledged for something that is very life threatening and something that's minor like a virus. They did a full investigation of everything he was struggling with, also in pictorial detail where they were most concerned. They did all the tests they needed to do, plus a scan. They booked an eye test and we got to uncover the situation.

It was disturbing at the eye appointment. The optometrist just looked very quietly at Jenson, and said, "Okay, he's such a smart boy, and he's so clever." She was getting him to read all the letters he could recognise and measuring the pressure behind his eyes, and then she just stopped.

I think that's when she started communicating with the consultant, because we'd been in there all day. It was clear by the expression on her face that something was not right. On her notes, I could make out the word "Urgent".

I called Adam at work and said, "I think you should come." I don't normally say things like that to him because I've normally got things covered on my own. I can manage. But I felt on this occasion, he needed to be there. So Adam left work early and came in halfway through the day.

He was concerned and realised how serious the situation was when I called him home urgently. My daughter was still at school so we would have to manage the day between us and take turns to look after our baby son Mason, who was only three months old. As a mother, I felt like I was not doing enough as there simply was not enough of me to go round.

Jenson was looking very pale and whilst we were waiting for his test results, he became incontinent, which was unusual, and sedentary. I was terrified. How much longer would we have to wait? Things were just not right.

He was feeling hungry though, but the doctors were insistent that he would be zero by mouth and could only have water. Of course, you do your best to adhere to this, but kids have a way of making you feel so bad that you get impatient and want answers.

By this time, I was on my own again. Adam had taken Mason home to collect some essentials for the hospital, and my daughter was at my friend's house as school had finished. I was playing with Jenson when the consultant came to speak to me.

She said, "Do you want to come through to the side room? I need to tell you what's happened with the scan."

Normally, when they say that, it's not good news. When you're put into the side room, it's because they don't want to say whatever it is in front of your child. Your heart flutters, then, you start to feel weak, with your legs buckling, and it's just very scary.

The nurses were so brilliant with Jenson. They kept him busy colouring in, doing funny pictures, and playing dressing up. They had very good instincts about what to do.

So, I went into the room. There was a still atmosphere, even our mobile phones weren't working properly. I had Adam's phone because my phone needed to be charged. So, that was the oddness of the situation. I had his phone. I sat down and the consultant sat there, and her doctor for the day was also sat there. She was looking quite upset and she just said, "I'm just terribly sorry, but he's got a brain tumour." It was so, so sad, because all I could think of was what the consultants were saying all day. The eye doctor was saying how smart he was, how he was getting everything so well, and he was just such a good boy, so happy. It was like she spoke in slow motion. A brain tumour. It took a few minutes to sink in.

I just remember screaming because I didn't have Adam there either, I was on my own. It was just such a massive blow, and I thought they'd just put a stick of dynamite in my family life and blown it up. I had no words, I had nothing to say. I just couldn't get any words out. I couldn't talk. The doctor was crying. I swear that they do show emotion. She'd got attached to Jenson because she'd been with him all day as well. I felt hollow, but most of all, numb with guilt. Why had I not taken him to the hospital sooner?

She said, "Well, the best thing we can do is get him to St. George's as soon as possible, because it's very serious and we need to get a surgeon as soon as we can."

From that moment, all I could think was, "How on earth, am I going to tell his Dad that his son has got a brain tumour. How am I going to make this phone call?" I had his phone as well, so it was so surreal.

Then his work mate from work called his phone and wanted to know where he was. I just said, "He's going to be away for a while. His son is very sick and I need to use the phone right now." He understood because of the seriousness of my voice to just leave it alone.

I hung up and then I had to phone Adam. I had to remember my landline number, which was just... "Oh my God, what is it?" I was shaking, I just couldn't do it. When he picked up, he was happy because he'd arranged everything to come back to the hospital. He was calm, like everything was under control.

He said, "I'm just heading back, just packing things up for Mason, getting all his milk ready." Then, he said, "Well, what happened? And how's it going?"

I just couldn't get the words out.

He said, "Well, what's wrong? Come on, you can do this. Just tell me what's happening."

Then I said, "He's got a brain tumour."

He just wailed out in so much pain. He kept saying, "No, no, no, this isn't right. This can't be happening. No, not my boy, not my little boy. Oh my God, what are we going to do?"

I said, "I don't know, we just need to get to the hospital. We need to get there tonight, and we just need to take essentials. Don't worry about all the extras, bring the kids. Just get here."

He just said, "Yes, yes, I'm getting into the car now right now. I'll be there as soon as I can."

We had to get organised amongst the chaos of this diagnosis. For some reason, my heart was telling me to stay calm and follow the medical advice as this was a life or death situation. As I waited with Jenson for the ambulance to arrive, I shed many more tears. Every now and then, I would get another cup of tea and just cry. I needed to be strong, but I had no clue how I was going to do this.

Looking back at all my son's milestones and health visitor appointments, nothing seemed out of place. He was meeting his targets and doing so with ease. He was a very bright and capable boy, and he found learning interesting. I can remember a few days before that fateful trip to the hospital when I took a tape measure and wrote down the measurement for his head circumference in his red book. I placed his measurement on the chart at way over 99% for his age. This didn't seem right to me and I was thinking about how his head felt tender to touch, almost as if it were stretched. I knew this was not normal. My instinct was telling me to get this checked. But I did not act on it. Jenson was incredibly tough, he never let anything get him down.

Jenson was being his usual happy self and just went off to play with his cars again. He never complained, he was not sick and did not have any seizures – the usual markers of a brain tumour. The only things that he had were fleeting headaches for about 30 seconds and a clumsy demeanour, often falling over like he'd caught his foot on something.

But Jenson had been trying to tell me he was unwell. He had been watching children's hospital programmes on TV. The whole Dr. Ranj obsession became clear, he needed our help. All the signs were there, but they were so subtle, nothing to catch your attention, just lurking, waiting to be found.

The sense of guilt kept echoing in my mind. Why didn't I take him to a doctor sooner? Why didn't I trust my instincts sooner? The only reasonable explanation I could come up with was that I had only just given birth to my youngest and that with the recovery from surgery, I had taken my eye off the ball. All my energy had been spent on healing myself so that I could keep up with the demands of family life.

The main thing I reminded myself was that I did take him to hospital and that he was now in the right place to get better. The nurses were great and made Jenson feel like he was having a fun day visiting the hospital, and they were always offering help when they could and that helped us stay calm.

Ambulance dash

Jenson and I were driven in the ambulance to the nearest neurosurgical unit, which was at St. George's hospital. The ambulance ride was like an adventure for Jenson. They made him feel like he was a VIP. The sirens were ringing loudly to clear the roads and, in fits of giggles, Jenson would say, "Again, again" as we raced along the motorway. He just held on to his teddy and looked to me for reassurance. That look gave me a sign of relief. It was like he was saying, "Thank you, Mum."

It was late when we arrived at St. Georges. Adam met us there with Mason and Sophia. Everyone was tired, and panicked and starving. It was time to prioritise, we needed food and rest.

When you are in this hospital environment, food is usually the last thing on your mind. In your mind, it feels like you will not be there for long. So, you hold on and stay by your child's side. No food passes your lips, but then the hours pass by and nurses start to offer you food and drink. They can see what you cannot. A couple of exhausted parents who need to keep their strength up.

We needed strength to endure the barrage of questions from the specialists who would visit Jenson every day. In the end, I had to make a timetable. We were working a full-time job with each assessment and scan being made, as well as managing a family. When you are a Mum to a young baby and older child, you need to plan how this will be okay for them. What do you need? Help and lots of it. I made some phone calls and, between us, we got our eldest daughter to school each day. With the love and support of our extended families and other parents, we were able to keep going. Those immediate days in hospital were the hardest, as we were facing the unknown. Would Jenson recover? What obstacles will lay ahead? Will he ever be the same again?

Neurosurgical unit

I felt like I had to repeat myself a lot, providing the information I had just given to the A&E team at the other hospital. From that point onwards, I knew that I would have to take careful notes of what was happening to Jenson to relay information to anyone who needed it within the hospital. This was the night I decided to become my son's project manager. I never asked for this job, but in this situation, I knew that if I didn't keep an eye on what was going on, we would soon become overwhelmed as a family.

I understood after the round of tests and form filling, and various questions about Jenson's childhood, that he had a low-grade, benign brain tumour attached to his brain stem. Second to this, he had acquired hydrocephalus. This is a build-up of fluid around the brain. Hydrocephalus if left untreated would have caused fatal damage to his brain, resulting in death. I needed to get a handle on the severity of the situation. We were incredibly lucky that he had managed for so long without having any seizures or sickness. The central nervous system bathes in cerebral spinal fluid (CSF for short) and if this cannot move freely in and around the brain, it can cause a variety of symptoms.

The doctors were shocked at how Jenson had been managing, because the way they explained, he only had a couple of weeks from it being fatal, either a fatal seizure or just complete... that's it, fatality.

It was something they couldn't comprehend. They asked me, "How did you know?" It's not like I knew, I said, it was more like an instinctive thing and that's why I brought him to the hospital. They just looked surprised, because he had so much fluid in his head, it must have been causing him so much pain. So, they decided to operate to try and relieve the pressure in there. It was traumatic because we didn't have enough time to process it. They were saying, we're going to do this, we're going to do that. We just had to go with it. It was like, "Oh, right. We've got to save his life, if it's a matter of life or death."

When it's a matter of life or death, it's easy to choose life. So you go with that.

"What's the outcome? Choose life. Yes. Okay. I will consent to the procedure. It's got to be that, it seems like our only option. That will save him."

Only one parent allowed

I remember them saying when we were there, "You can't all stay together, you're only allowed one parent and the child in the room, as there's not enough room for everyone."

That made me even more upset, because, obviously, I didn't want to be away from Mason either, because he was still very young and needed me. So, we had to try and arrange things ourselves there and then. It was midnight, maybe one o'clock in the morning. We were in the waiting room trying to work out sleeping arrangements. Eventually, Adam was able to get through to his sister, who lived 45 minutes away, and he managed to take Sophia and Mason there for the evening. He was distraught, he didn't want to go, he didn't want to be apart from Jenson, because he just didn't know what was going to go on.

When you're in that volatile state, you're just so emotional and whatever anyone's saying to you, you're not taking it in. At the same time, you just want to be heard. We really felt as a family that we weren't being heard. It just felt unfair that we couldn't all be together. And so Adam and the children spent that night at his sister's. Each night that I was apart from Mason felt awful. As a new Mum, my hormones were in overdrive. I could not stop crying.

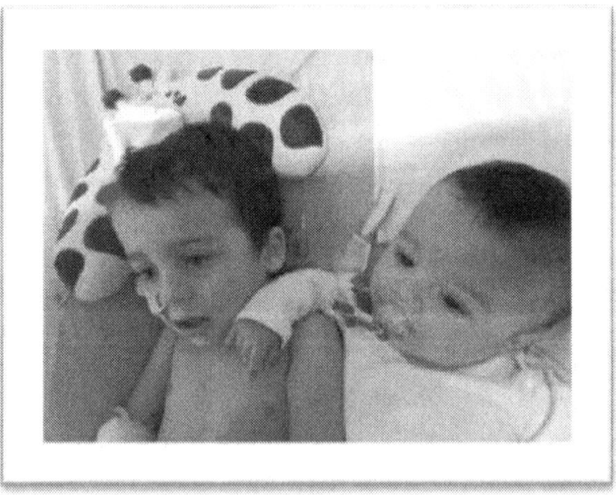

The next day the procedure to release the fluid from his brain went smoothly. Jenson came out of his surgery a happier little boy. But the doctors said the big operation, the one they were going to do in a few days' time to get the tumour out, would be the longest operation. They showed me a picture of the tumour, which was the size of a plum or a golf ball. It was huge having anything like that in the head.

They asked me again, "How on earth, would you have known it? You said that he didn't show typical brain tumour symptoms like vomiting or heavy seizures?"

He didn't have those things. He had those brief headaches, but they could have been normal. What was remarkable was, how did I know that there was something going on? Still to this day, I can't answer that. It was just a very strong instinct, a willingness and I guess a determination to find out what was going on, to find an answer and not be fobbed off.

I think there are many occasions you could be fobbed off and reassured it's nothing major by your GP or a healthcare professional, and you would accept it, but it was my reluctance to accept any of that and to just push through that got me where I needed to be. I felt a sense of urgency that I needed to do it, that I needed to push. Normally, I'm quite a calm person, and I would just say, "Okay, I get what you're saying", playing down the situation. But on this occasion, I was nothing like that. I had to push everybody to get the answer. And then, when it hit home what it was, it felt like being wounded, severely wounded, just having no air. It felt like I couldn't articulate any words. It was just one of those freeze responses, when you're in shock.

There was nothing I could do to change the situation. It was something that was out of my hands and in the hands of the surgeon. I had to have that level of trust with him. He is one of the best surgeons they have, with 20 years of paediatric surgical experience, especially brain and neurological surgery. Jenson was in the best pair of hands there.

The neurosurgeon said, "Yes, I am preparing. I will be at my best. I'll take care of him." He had that calmness about him and I really appreciated it. When I asked him to show me his hands, they were still. The slightest tremble in surgery would be devastating to Jenson.

I looked him in the eye. I've never been so serious in all my life, and I said, "Make sure you bring him back to me. Make sure we bring him back."

I was looking at the paperwork and it was just saying all the things that could happen, all the risks, and all I could think about was him being alive. So, I didn't read every single letter, because at that moment, all I wanted was for him to be alive. So, I signed the consent form.

I said, "Go get this thing out. We've got to get this thing out. You know, there isn't any other choice."

The surgeon said, "There isn't. This is the way it's positioned. I'm going to do as much as I can to take it out and we can review the outcome from there."

A few brief days of normality

It is not every day that you ask for these things, and it seemed like I was asking for a lot. The next day, I wanted to take Jenson home for the weekend. I just had this urge to spend some time with him and just do some silly things, just play and just enjoy him whilst he was feeling a bit better. Now that he'd had that fluid removed, we'd got him back. He had loads of energy, and I really liked that. I watched him giggling and having fun.

He was feeling a bit groggy after the anaesthetic, but he was back to being Jenson. I just wanted to take him home for a few days of normality. The doctors didn't want me to take him out of hospital. So, I had to have an argument with them and state the case as to why I wanted him home.

I said, "Well, he's going in for major brain surgery, and we don't know what the outcome will be from that. I think whilst I have him like this, I just want to spend a bit of time with him."

It was almost like they didn't want to trust me because they thought I wouldn't be responsible enough to look after him. I just reminded them that I'd brought him to them because I knew there was something wrong with him. So I'd been responsible the whole time.

I said, "Please give me all medication that you've given him and I'll make sure he takes it at the right time. I just need the weekend with him."

They eventually agreed. It took four hours for them to come to the conclusion that I could do it, and that he could be discharged, because hospital discharges take so, so long.

We left the hospital that night, and as we drove back from London, we could see foxes playing on the lawns of people's gardens. It was so late, it was one in the morning before we got home. We were used to getting up in these early hours in the mornings and so it didn't matter. I think we were just happy that we could have Jenson home for the weekend. So, when we got home, we put him to bed and just watched him, feeling incredibly grateful. I think that was key. Just being very grateful for who Jenson was and all his personality traits. Obviously, we were grateful to be with Mason, feeding him, making sure he was on track. He seemed pretty good, he was filling out and getting bigger. We just enjoyed looking at our family and loving the whole situation we had.

Even though it was painful, because we knew it wasn't going to stay this way, and there was this heartbreak underneath it all, we tried to keep it as normal as possible. Jenson didn't know any better. He was just playing around because he had this new energy and there was no pressure in his head. He was able to stand properly and he was hopping on one leg.

I thought, "Wow, we've not seen that for a long, long time." And we captured these videos of him doing it, dressed as a pumpkin, because it was Halloween.

It was great to see him having a bit of fun and his sister joining in. They played together nicely, dressed in their Halloween costumes. It was just like the build-up, like the calm before the storm, not knowing what was going to happen afterwards. In that situation, you just tread water and wait for the next wave to come and hit you.

The phone call I'd had the previous day from the hospital felt like a warning. It was the way the Clinical Nurse Specialist worded it, that put doubt in my head. From the beginning, I'd always been instinctively sure that I was on the right track, that I was choosing the right thing by Jenson. I'd been guided that this was the best thing for him, but when she called and said, "We won't know the full consequences of this action, until after the procedure", I felt scared .

"What do you mean by consequences?"

There was an overload of information. There were loads of forms to fill in. I was tired but I tried to remember everything that it said in the leaflet they gave me. The obvious one is that some kids die after an operation like that, because it's so life threatening. That one came straight to my mind. You don't want to be even thinking about that before your child has an operation. I started reeling off all the really serious consequences, including stroke, but none of them seemed too bad, considering he'd be alive. So, I stuck to what I had decided, which was that we would go ahead with this surgery.

I was mentally preparing for that, and we thought we were ready for it. I was trying to get everything arranged family wise. We had to make sure with the baby that we had everything he needed. We travelled so light, we just literally had one bag with enough nappies, one bottle, a couple of baby grows, changing gear, and that was it. I didn't really pack for anything longer than a few days, because we didn't really know what would happen.

The surgeon said, if the surgery goes well, Jenson would spend a couple of weeks in intensive care based on his recollection of other procedures he'd done in the past. We had no reason to doubt that it would be any different for us.

MRIs, CTs and X-Rays

To enable the neurosurgeons to make a clinical diagnosis, they needed to perform a variety of scans to visually capture the location and potential grade of Jenson's tumour. MRIs offered the most detail information, without surgical intervention. Jenson had several CT scans and, with each one, they could get a better understanding of what was going on in his brain. The downside to this was the radiation exposure. Each scan would expose Jenson to a small quantity of radiation, which if they kept repeating the scans could encourage tumour growth. This is what I feel may have happened to Jenson post-operatively as he was regularly checked for a variety of symptoms. Jenson's low-grade benign tumour was the size of a small plum, sitting at the back of his brain and affecting his balance and co-ordination. The surgeon looked quietly confident that he could remove the whole mass without the need for further treatment. However, when the scan came back, he noticed that the tumour originated from the brain stem, a part of the brain where you cannot operate. Quite simply, in most books, it will read "damage to the brain stem will lead to incompatibility with life" or, in other words, death.

Faced with the real prospect that they may not be able to fully remove the tumour was another devastating blow. Yet, somehow, I was able to have a highly logical conversation about preserving the good parts of his brain. Our surgeon fully appreciated this and gave us hope that if we could get all this tumour out, Jenson would fully recover and lead a normal life. For some reason, I had to have this piece of information, as it gave me hope and a positive attitude towards the surgery. We did not have many options or time to wait and see. His brain was losing some cognitive functions and if we did not act quickly, we would lose him. So, with this, it was easy. I chose surgery... but that was only the start of this battle. With each decision we made, there were always consequences, and these would not be known until many weeks later.

Takeaway: Less common symptoms to look out for

Jenson didn't display the usual symptoms that would indicate a tumour, such as seizures and sickness. The symptoms I noticed were:

1) **Double vision** or pulling objects close to his eyes. Jenson would do this with his cars, and although it was an odd thing to do, it was his way of being able to see the details of the wheels, the colours and the bodywork. He would lay his head to one side and watch how they moved across his desk.

2) **Not looking up or being able to look at things above his head.** He would feel dizzy and would often wobble backwards. The sudden change of looking up and down would cause him distress. This was caused by the fluid building up in his brain altering the pressure behind the eyes. This pressure would have caused some intense headaches – the kind of headaches he had for short intervals of 30 seconds, where he would scream and hold his head, as if he had bumped it on something.

3) **Not being able to jump.** After Jenson's two-year health check, it was odd that he did not develop the motor skills for jumping with both feet off the ground. The health visitors reassured me that this was nothing to worry about and that all children develop at different rates. What I noticed was that he could not hop or lift one leg off the ground without feeling disorientated.

4) **Becoming reclusive.** Not having the desire to be outdoors anymore and feeling the need to be close to me. Jenson loved playing on his balance bike and

scooter. He was such an outdoor kid. He loved the muddy puddles on rainy days and using the playground before pre-school. Nothing was a challenge. He was brave and attempted everything. When this changed and he no longer liked these things, I started to question whether everything was okay.

5) **Enlarged head circumference.** It was by chance that I had a tape measure one morning after his first day at pre-school. I thought I would update his little Red Book. After taking the data and plotting it on the graph, it did not look right. Jenson was on the 99th percentile. This was abnormal and needed to be checked. Doctors will always take your concerns on board if you have enough evidence to suggest that something is not right with your child. By gathering all these observations and pieces of data and presenting it to the doctors, they were able to investigate the right clinical pathway to his diagnosis.

Takeaway: Trust your instincts

What to do to back up your suspicions:

1) Take notice of what your child is trying to tell you. For example, Jenson kept watching 'Dr. Ranj' on TV and mentioned how he felt like "wobbly jelly". Taking these factors into consideration will help you understand. Not every child can articulate the correct words to explain what is wrong, but they can show you through their behaviour.

2) Keep an observation diary of anything that may look out of the ordinary. It was my logical recollection of symptoms and how they could be linked that lead to a correct diagnosis of a brain tumour. Doctors and medical professionals really appreciate any information that you can give them as it saves time and directs them to the most effective treatment.

3) Do not listen to other's opinions. If you feel that something is wrong, then act, call the doctor or the emergency department for urgent advice. When your parents get involved, it can cause all sorts of emotions and complete co-dependency that they will somehow have all the answers for you. Believe me, your instinct is telling you all that you need to know. So be prepared to go against what they may say. This can cause friction and arguments, but deep down you know that this is the right decision. Trust yourself.

4) Reflecting on these things, it now seems obvious that something was going on with Jenson's head. However, with the complications of family life and the school runs, we rarely had time to act upon these suspicions. Timing was everything and my reactions to the situation helped

Jenson to get the help he needed before it was too late. Never underestimate your instincts, it was instinct that allowed me to save my son from death.

Chapter 2: Surgery or in some cases Multiple Surgeries

A steep learning curve

Sometimes it is hard to comprehend how such a young boy could endure so many procedures within a short space of time. Even now looking back over the last four years, he amazes me with the sheer strength he possesses to merely get the job done!

Early on, before deciding on the right course of action to take, the neurosurgeons had to create a way to drain the excess fluid accumulating in Jenson's brain (relieving pressure). The hydrocephalus was a secondary condition to the primary tumour diagnosis. Because the tumour had blocked the ability for the fluid to drain naturally, a man-made one had to be created to help Jenson re-establish a normalised feel to his brain – easing the nausea, headache and unsteadiness. This surgery would take a couple of hours under anesthetic.

While this was the first surgery, it most certainly would not be the last. If you ever feel terrible about signing consent forms, you need to find a way to cope with the potential guilt if things do go wrong. In my case, this did not necessarily hit me until a week later, whilst signing a consent form for the invasive brain surgery that would take our team at St. Georges six hours to complete.

An endoscopic third ventriculostomy is a procedure that involves making a hole through the third ventricle to allow the drainage of CSF into the spinal cord. The brain and spinal cord bathe in this fluid and it is regularly drained at about a pint a day. So, you can imagine the effect of this fluid being blocked. It placed pressure behind Jenson's eyes and the immense pressure inflicted pain in his head, making him unable him to look up or jump. We were not to know that this was going on as the tumour behaved like an iceberg hidden in the calm waters. This procedure was performed within a couple of hours under anaesthetic. For me and Adam, this was terrifying as we'd never had to go through anything like this with Jenson before. When he closed his eyes as he went under, I felt like I was not going to see him again. I could not even talk. I had a lump in my throat and was choking back the tears. The surgeon was superb, he had such an aura of calm that I felt like Jenson was in safe hands. I had to let go and trust he would bring my boy back to fight another day.

Guilt became my norm. Everything I turned to look at, my children, house, career, partner and relatives, made me feel like I'd let everyone down. I felt shame at not being able to act sooner, even after having a consolatory chat with the surgeon, who appeared astonished at how I knew what it was, and how close Jenson was to a fatal seizure.

The surgeon said with some authority, "You were definitely right, you didn't have two weeks, otherwise Jenson wouldn't be here."

In his small room, I found a source of comfort, knowing that I was in the right place, surrounded by an army of medical professionals.

I must admit, when I realised that we would be transferred to London, I did not think the neurosurgical team would be as brilliant as they were. For sure, we had our moments when things went wrong and Jenson had to be urgently treated, but for the most part, they worked incredibly hard. The way that they took the time to explain what had happened and how the procedures would work was invaluable, as we were putting our most precious person in their hands. We wanted our Jenson back, whatever it took, we just simply could not think of the alternative. It was too unbearable to think about.

Two hours later, a grumpy Jenson was sat up in bed with a little patch on his head. All he could think of was food and boy did he want to eat. It was just a shame that those steroids had other ideas. The interaction of the anaesthetic and medication made for chronic vomiting and diarrhea, which gave the nurses and me some serious work to do. This job was not for the faint-hearted and needed a strong stomach. Caring for Jenson through this period was difficult as he could not just go home, he had to do as he was told and stay in bed.

However, when we were allowed and the observations were okay, I made a mission to get him discharged, so that we could spend the weekend together as a family before the big operation. In hindsight, this was an incredibly wise decision, as we were able to prepare ourselves and remember Jenson as he was before our lives changed forever. Sometimes, you need to speak up and be insistent about what you want. In this case for us, we were willing to take on the responsibilities of giving him his medication and checking his observations regularly.

When you show you can do this, the doctors will support you, as they can see the benefit it will have for the family. To sit back and allow the impending situation to overwhelm you will remove your ability to make decisions. As a family, we did everything together and this was a way I could involve my other children, so that they knew what was going on. I could prepare them for the challenges that lay ahead and reassure them that Mum and Dad were going to be helping Jenson to get better. It was important that my daughter understood that I was not going to be gone forever but just for a little while and that we could spend time together at the weekends, whilst Jenson was in hospital. Thinking back now, this was an effective way of communicating, as we were there for far longer than we could ever imagine.

It was supposed to be successful

Taking that long drive with both of the boys in the back of the car felt numb. No words were spoken but lots of fun games were played to keep the energy flowing. Jenson was asking about football and Mason babbled in response, usually this meant that he had filled his nappy. The roads were clear and nothing seemed to trouble us apart from that deep seated fear of what if? We wanted Jenson to be well again and the tumour to be removed without any problems. But that phone call and the discussion of consequences never left my mind. As we approached the car park Jenson knew we were going to sort out his poorly head. He didn't feel frightened but there was a scared look on his face.

We figured out where we needed to go and sat there in the waiting area, anxiously waiting for our surgeon to arrive and talk through the procedure. It was midday and Jenson had not eaten a thing since he woke at 6am. He was starting to get annoyed. We tried to distract him but he was getting bored and Mason wanted to get out and have a roll around the floor on his playmat. Every now and then a wave of fear would come over Adam, he would fidget and keep moving around. At some point a nurse offered him a chance to buy some raffle tickets for a luxury holiday in Portugal. This was a welcomed distraction He purchased two and that took about five minutes off the waiting time. Waiting, waiting, waiting it was building up a level of anxiety I had never experienced before. At some points of the Day I would be fine, others I wanted to just leave with Jenson and not go through with the surgery.

Then one of the nurses tracked down a play specialist, who came through with a football and bubble mixture. As Jenson was tearing up and down the corridor of the children's ward with the football, the surgeon was going through all the paperwork and anaesthetics came in to discuss how they would put Jenson to sleep. The team were ready at two o'clock, it was time to go down, it was time to say goodbye to Jenson and hope for the best that he will survive this dangerous operation.

The brain surgery was supposed to be successful and it was in terms of what they did. After five or six hours later. We were told to go and meet Jenson as he was back and in intensive care. I had bought Jenson some pyjamas and hospital bedding to make him feel more comfortable. I had some Spider Man slippers that lit up when you walked on the floor. These would be perfect. The talk with the surgeon was sobering, they had done all they could and Jenson coped well with the operation. But they could not remove all of his tumour as it was too dangerous. Jenson would require further treatment and monitoring. This was awful, but hopeful at the same time. A feeling we would get all too familiar with. But they weren't bargaining on something so serious happening afterwards.

So three days in, you think, okay, things are okay, but they're not, and then everything shuts down. The last thing I heard Jenson say was that he couldn't see. He asked where his sister was. Then he stopped talking. He said, "Where's Sophia?" and then that was it. Those were his last words. It was just mad. I tried to get him to talk. Nothing, nothing at all. His whole body just shut down and it's hard to describe it. He was so still, it was like his soul had left his body. His heart rate slowed. I thought, "What the hell is going on here. What's happened to him. He's not supposed to deteriorate after surgery. He's supposed to be getting better."

None of the medical team had any answers. None of them. They were all concerned and they wanted to do more with his medicine, give him morphine and things like that.

I said, "Well, do you think that's a good idea? Considering he's already barely breathing. He's just very still, I mean, this isn't normal. Can I talk to somebody about this?"

They were going, "Oh, it needs time. We need to give him time to come around."

I said, "I don't think this is about time. I think something bad has just happened."

I had to grab hold of one of the consultants in intensive care. Not the nurses or registrars a senior doctor as I felt no one was listening. Panicking, I was pressing the call button and flagging down any consultants I could get hold of. Eventually I managed to get hold of one. She was an Italian lady. She was very strong willed and had a great character. She came over to see Jenson and she was talking to him but he wasn't responding or anything.

She tried to lift his arms up. Then she said, "Oh my God, what's going on with his right side. Nothing's happening."

She was trying to get him to react to some physical tests, but he couldn't do anything. She was concerned. So he had to have a lot of intensive scans. They were checking to see if something else had happened. They came back with nothing really. They were saying that there was bruising in his brain.

They didn't pick up on the fact that maybe his stitches weren't holding and he was having pressure building up. They didn't pick up on anything like that until three days later. It was just one thing after another. And as a mother, you're watching it and you're just horrified by it.

At no point did they say that a condition such as posterior fossa syndrome was a thing that could happen. I had to earwig as mums do, we have a good sense of multitasking. We can hear someone across the road, whilst we are still pushing a buggy around, and this served me well in this environment, because I heard one of the specialist nurses mention this condition. She was across the room, so she didn't think I could hear anything she was saying. I'd never heard of it before. That was the thing that stuck in my head, apart from all this horrific stuff that was happening in front of me, with my son barely moving or anything. It was hard, but I had to research the condition whilst I was there in intensive care.

Desperate sadness of the intensive care lounge

I remember staying in the intensive care lounge. It had these awful green leather sofas. There was nothing in there remotely comfortable. You needed to bring your own things because they didn't have anything for tea, coffee, even basic things for making of a hot drink, just water. I don't know whether there were problems with the toilet, but it was just horrendous. It stank. All these parents staying in the lounge were traumatised, because their kids were seriously ill and some of them might not even make it. And we're made to stay in accommodation that bad. I just sat in there. I thought, what is going on, there's got to be better accommodation than this. I had to be there for that night and it's not something you want to ever sit through. But as Adam and I were taking turns, going in and out to see Jenson throughout the night, another family came in and their son was not doing very well. I think he was dying. They gathered everybody into the reception waiting area and the mother was very upset. But when you sit there, you feel like you're invading their space. There's no privacy. She needed her space. I think it was two in the morning. She came in and just screamed and then collapsed to the floor. I sat up, thinking, "Wow, what's going on?" Then I realised what had happened. Her son had died and all the family were crying. It was unbearably sad, because you are upset yourself. There were a couple of other parents there with kids who were seriously ill and we had nowhere to go.

I wanted to help them, but I just didn't know what to do for the best, because she was inconsolable. The worst thing – I suppose it's part of their job – was the doctors coming in and giving the mother a leaflet about what to do next. I just thought, "Wow, that just seems so insensitive that it comes down to just having a bit of paper given to you and the curtain pulled round your child." I went back into the ward to see Jenson and the curtain was pulled round their child. All the kids there would have been aware of what was happening and it would have been shocking for them. Thankfully, Jenson was on the other side of the ward, so he wouldn't have seen it all. But for me, that was something that I'll never forget.

It shook me up. If you're ever in that sort of desperate situation where something's happened unexpectedly and you have to experience it, it is soul destroying. I really felt for that family. You know, if they could have been a bit more compassionate to them, it would have gone a long way because it was obvious that English wasn't their first language either. It was very hard for the mother to understand what was going to happen. She looked so scared and frightened. I think that sort of came across to everyone else, because when the family left in the early hours of the morning to take a break and eat something, everyone was upset. We'd been holding it together well in that meeting room for a couple of days, but it just all went to shit.

Everyone was just in floods of tears. The other parents there – I knew their son had cancer and was fighting for his life – were having a hard day. And we were having a hard day generally, just having to stomach the fact that Jenson was going to be in the hospital for a very long time. It was not going to be a couple of weeks, like the surgeon had initially quoted. I don't even think he realised the enormity of what had happened. So when I was rereading my journal, it reminded me of the depth of sadness in that room, it was just an indescribable pain. You just want to take it away from them. You wish you could do something to help them. That really hurt me, even though it wasn't my child.

I just thought, "how life can be so cruel, our children did not deserve this. Why was this happening?" The desire to get out of that room was urgent. Then, when I went back onto the ward, one of the nurses said, "I've called in a favour with one of the guys at Ronald McDonald House and they've managed to make a room available for you."

I said, "Brilliant." I just went from being immensely sad to elated within sixty seconds. I was crying because I was deeply saddened by the recent events. Then I was crying because I was happy, because we'd actually had a breakthrough. We had accommodation where we could all be together. I can't even begin to describe the relief. It was like champagne bubbles. Even though I felt so sad for everyone else, it was an important breakthrough for us.

Ronald McDonald House

The Ronald McDonald House charity aims to help every child in hospital to have their families close by, and to ensure their families are fully supported in their Ronald McDonald House and remain actively involved in their child's care.

While Jenson was in intensive care, Adam and the kids had to come and go as there wasn't enough room for everyone to stay at the hospital. We stressed the urgency of having somewhere to stay as Mason needed to be with me, but the hospital had policies that didn't reflect our family situation and needed to be challenged. The Clinical Nurse Specialist realised this and made a call to Ronald McDonald House situated within the hospital grounds. It was fortunate that we managed to get a room that would be sufficient for my other children and comfortable enough to sleep in. I was exhausted and feeding Mason was important to me, but I just couldn't keep going. We had to switch to formula bottles, so that Adam could take over and take Mason out of the hospital for parts of the day. My daughter stayed with Adam's parents, which was a tough decision for me as this wasn't something I wanted to do, but it was important for her to keep to a routine to reduce anxiety and keep her schoolwork on track. Jenson was going to be in hospital for months, so getting this sorted out sooner rather than later was essential.

My family were amazing, they all took turns to come and visit us in hospital. My brother brought along a survival kit consisting of snacks, toiletries and magazines. My Mum offered to take my daughter for a week, which she really loved. Nanny was her favourite person to be around and that gave her some comfort, while we were trying to work things out. Mason had to play with Jenson in hospital, while we were waiting for all his results and consultant checks. He never really had the chance to go to any baby groups, it just wasn't possible. However, he was thriving, and he looked strong and healthy. This gave Jenson some hope too, seeing his little brother getting bigger each day. Schools will never tell you if your child is struggling, but Sophia's did. One day she just fell apart and cried uncontrollably, "I want my brother back." All I could do was reassure her that we were doing the best we could do. It broke me inside to hear that she missed me so much and hated staying away from us. So when I told her the good news that she could come and stay at the weekends at the Ronald McDonald House, she threw her arms around me. Clearly, she needed me and I knew that we needed this place to keep everyone together.

From: Pillay Strinivasa
Sent: 30 August 2022 14:55
To: Kimberley Shamtally
Cc: Slater Emily
Subject: RE: Your Story

Hi Kim, it was great catching up with you yesterday.

As per our conversation please see my testimony below. I will not be around until next Friday after today, so if you have anything you would like to ask Emily my colleague would be happy to help.

"It was my personal pleasure, as well as that of the whole team at Ronald McDonald House Tooting, to meet Jenson's parents, Kim and Adam, as well as his older sister XXXX, later on. From my first impressions, and like so many of the families who'd come before them, they were good people, who had had a life-changing situation thrust upon them and who needed our support as a Charity and as a team.

Kim and Adam were very happy that they could have "normal" conversations with the team; it took them away from the pressure of their situation. It helped them maintain a sense of normality which they had lost. Ronald McDonald House Charities UK's 13 Houses around the UK are run by dedicated teams, who endeavor to do their very best to engage with families and offer them unrivaled support throughout their stay. Kim mentioned to me that she does not think it was a coincidence that the first time Jenson spoke after being admitted, was at the Tooting House. Many families who bring their children over to the House from the hospital ward have spoken of the positive difference it seems to make to their child's happiness and sense of security. Our communal spaces, which include the kitchen, dining room, playroom, lounges and garden, allowed Kim and Adam to have family to visit. This, in turn, gave them the extra support they needed to make it through the toughest days.

A trip to Hamleys on Regent Street was arranged for the family, which brightened up their time no end, Jenson's eldest sister was reportedly 'taken aback' by the size and scale of the iconic toy retailer. The special treat allowed them to have some much needed quality time together. Kim also spoke fondly of her memories of Christmas spent at the House, with other incredibly strong and resilient families in similarly challenging situations, many of whom have become lifelong friends.

Each family is precious to us. In 2021, Ronald McDonald House Charities UK accommodated 3916 families living, on average, 62 miles away, saving each family around £1240 during their stay at a House. A lot of families say how much less stressed they feel, knowing that for as long as their child is in hospital, they have a safe space to stay."

Kindest regards,

Strini.

Strini Pillay
House Assistant
Ronald McDonald House Charities
Direct line: 0208 682 7625

St George's Hospital, Blackshaw Road, Tooting SW17 0QT

Hi Kim, it was great catching up with you yesterday.

As per our conversation please see my testimony below. I will not be around until next Friday after today, so if you have anything you would like to ask Emily my colleague would be happy to help.

It was my personal pleasure, as well as that of the whole team at Ronald McDonald House Tooting to meet Jenson's parents, Kim and Adam, as well as his older sister on From my first impressions, and like so many of the families who'd come before them, they were good people, who had had a life-changing situation thrust upon them and who needed our support as a Charity and as a team

Kim and Adam were very happy that they could have "normal" conversations with the team, it took them away from the pressure of their situation. It helped them maintain a sense of normality which they had lost. Ronald McDonald House Charities UK's 13 Houses around the UK are run by dedicated teams, who endeavor to do their very best to engage with families and offer them unrivaled support throughout their stay. Kim mentioned to me that she does not think it was a coincidence that the first time Jenson spoke after being admitted, was at the Tooting House. Many families who bring their children over to the House from the hospital ward have spoken of the positive difference it seems to make to their child's happiness and sense of security. Our communal spaces, which include the kitchen, dining room, playroom, lounges and garden, allowed Kim and Adam to have family to visit. This, in turn, gave them the extra support they needed to make it through the toughest days.

A trip to Hamleys on Regent Street was arranged for the family, which brightened up end, Jenson's eldest sister was reportedly taken aback by the size and scale of the iconic toy retailer. The special treat allowed them to have some much-needed quality time together im also spoke fondly of her memories of Christmas spent at the House, with other incredibly strong and resilient families in similarly challenging situations, many of whom have become lifelong friends the toughest days.

A trip to Hamleys on Regent Street was arranged for the family, which brightened up their time no end, Jenson's eldest sister was reportedly taken aback by the size and scale of the iconic toy retailer. The special treat allowed them to have some much-needed quality time together. Kim also spoke fondly of her memories of Christmas spent at the House, with other incredibly strong and resilient families in similarly challenging situations, many of whom have become lifelong friends.

Each family is precious to us. In 2021, Ronald McDonald House Charities UK accommodated 3916 families living, on average, 62 miles away, saving each family around £1240 during their stay at a House. A lot of families say how much less stressed they feel, knowing that for as long as their child is in hospital, they have a safe space to stay."

Kindest regards,

Strini

Strini Pillay
House Assistant
Ronald McDonald House Charities
Direct line: 0208 682 7625

St George's Hospital, Blackshaw Road, Tooting SW17 OQT

Time for a plan of action, not sadness

After we moved into Ronald McDonald House, I was quietly thinking to myself, this is it. This is where things get a bit better, because if I can have my family together in that room, we've got more chance of sticking this out. Up until that moment,

I'd thought that me and Adam were going to split up because this was too much stress. I'd only just had Mason. I didn't even have a clue if he was going to be okay and bond with me through this experience. Because it was just like a bomb had gone off in the whole family situation. Would my daughter be as close to me as she was before? It just seemed like a very impossible task. How were things ever going to be the same again?

The simple answer is, they weren't. So I had to make a plan in my mind. This is day one of how we sort through each problem rather than just wallow in this emotion of sadness. I couldn't act on sadness. I couldn't even get out of bed. In that state, you can't brush your teeth, you can't do your hair or your make-up. I didn't even know where my make-up was at this point. Caring for myself had become bottom of the list. I had to do something about it, but you're so blinkered when you're that down, you just don't put yourself first. You're last. Everyone else comes first, especially Jenson. I was at the hospital all the time. I was hyper vigilant watching him each micro minute of my day. The nurses were always telling me to go and get something to eat, to go and get a drink.

But because I'm so stubborn – I don't know where Jenson gets it from – I just sat there. The nurse would ask me if I'd like a drink. "Okay, I'll have a tea." Then they'd bring me a drink.

The nurse would say, "We got you a sandwich. Do you want to eat your sandwich?"

I'd say, "I will eat it in a minute."

She'd insist, "Not a lot's going to happen between now and in half an hour. He's fine."

It was just that I had no appetite. I had no appetite or desire. It was just gone. So you try and eat when you don't want to. It's just a strange scenario and you want to reject everything. I appreciated the nurses giving me a drink or a sandwich, but I wasn't acknowledging anything. This was the phase I was in when we moved into Ronald McDonald House, not knowing how long it was going to be for.

We didn't even know what our son had and whether he was going to be okay. There were so many questions and uncertain circumstances. You kind of have to be kind to yourself and go, well, we've got this far, let's see what happens the next day.

I think it's what people call faith. You have to believe it's going to turn around and get better. But my instincts hadn't turned off because of this massive shock. They'd got even more heightened by it. So I was acting on them a lot more through doing journaling, where I was writing up the day's events and how I was feeling every evening. It kind of brought up those emotions of unease about certain things they were doing in the hospital and things like that. I guess I got courage. I wasn't brave. I just got courage. I just started asking questions.

I wasn't afraid anymore. I started to ask questions and some of the medical staff didn't even know the answer. I asked the neurosurgeon. He didn't know. At least he was being honest, but it was a start of something, like a catalyst for change. Because the more questions I asked, the more momentum I got to be able to look at things logically. Where are we going with this? This is long term now. It's not short term. He's not going to spontaneously come back. All correct. Like before he went into surgery, kicking a ball about. No, no, no. Let's accept that now. Cry it all out, which I did.

Gosh, there was a lot of crying. I went over to his bed and just cried, and the nurses said, "Wow, we've got to work together."

I said, "I fully appreciate that, but my heart is broken. I am broken right now. So can you just leave me alone? Just get out all of you, right now."

In that moment, I thought, "I've got to be different because this isn't going to help Jenson. It's not going to help me. It's not going to help anyone." So I just had to suck it up. This is the shit. Yep. Things aren't going to be the same, I accept that. I guess this is grief right now because I've lost him. This is him, but it's not him. My job now is to get to know Jenson, because he's still in there, it's just that at the moment, he's not himself.

So all these things whirled around in my head, so I could make sense of it. It is painful because you don't expect to do that with someone who's still alive. When someone dies, you expect the ceremony and you say your goodbyes. But when they're in front of you and they're still there, and they're looking for help and whatever you can do for them, but you're so distraught about the one you've lost, it's a horrible situation. You've got to go in everyday and you've got to try and do your best. I thought, "What can I do that would be good for him, that he needs? I'm a therapist. Why don't I just become his employee and work with him and change hats, become professional and detach from the mother bit just to get a handle on it?"

I suppose that sounds cold, but the detachment made sense, because I was able to think properly, about what I could do, all the good stuff that I'd been doing for years with my clients, and how I could gather together a programme of things we could do every day. There are so many hours in a day. You can't just sit there watching 24 hours a day in hospital. You've got to do something to carve the day up. So I made a timetable – well, they actually gave me this daily timetable. We put in all Jenson's appointments and got organised. This was a step forward. Okay. So Monday, Tuesday, Wednesday, he's got the physio and occupational therapist, and the speech and language therapist.

He's got the consultant paediatrician. There were so many people involved, from dieticians to ophthalmologists, just everything went into the timetable.

When the doctors come in to see your child, you can do other activities with them. You can practise movements, but you have to make it more fun. So I introduced toys and behaved silly, and was just engaging, using laughter to try and get some response from Jenson, to make sure he was getting it. Every day, I'd bring Mason in on purpose, because he was cuddly. He'd got to the cuddly six-month phase. He was just baby cute, with big, chunky legs. He was full of fun. I thought, "He's going to wind up his brother, isn't he? So let's just put pure joy next to Jenson and see what happens." I put Mason next to Jenson and he'd be flicking his legs around trying to do things. Jenson was looking at him out of the corner of his eye.

Jenson kept looking at Mason, like he was thinking, "Why is he still there?" I said, "I put Mason in there next to you." We played a game and I thought, "Well, let's see, I've got a little baby comb that was Mason's, and I put it on the top of Jenson's head. Obviously, he didn't like that very much. Then all of a sudden, his arm moved, he wanted to take it off, he wiped it off his head. I thought, "Wow, look at that? You moved." It was just the engagement of Mason lying next him. So I thought, well, that's kind of working. We need to do that more. And it became a thing. We would just do play time and the more Jenson engaged, the better he felt, and it made such a big change to everybody. There was more optimism. So with that, we could work forward in terms of how we were going to cope, because when you're in hospital, everything medical is essentially done for you.

You've got people holding your hand all the time, and there's the sheer horror of being left on your own with all these things to look after and not having a single clue how to do it. It's just too frightening to comprehend. But knowing that he could move a bit was hopeful. So it was good. And Mason was a big part of it, being a baby and just knowing no better. He was the catalyst for Jenson to just have a go. Brotherly love. Do I love you or hate you? You could see in his face that he was starting to get a bit of expression back. Half of his lip would go up and I was like, "Ooh, you're coming back, Jenson, we're annoying you enough. We'll just have a break and come back later."

Keeping the family together

So it was a hard time trying to keep family together, because the nurses and the doctors were always explaining about the lack of ward space and such, and I was trying to appreciate that.

But at the same time, I had to put my foot down and go, "I need to see my family today. This isn't a situation we wanted to be in and it's not one that a lot of people find themselves in. So it's a two-way thing. If you could allow us this time so we can be together, and do story time and things like that, then it will make it easier for Jenson. Because he's finding it hard too, he hasn't seen his friends. He hasn't been anywhere for weeks and he thinks he's just going to be here forever. That in itself must be frightening for him."

So for once I wasn't thinking of me. I was actually thinking about how he must be looking at it and that was something new, because up to that point, we hadn't even thought of what it must be like for him.

Then he got a card from his preschool. They sent it to the hospital and it was from all his friends. They made little pictures, but he was just not feeling it. So he just turned away. It was a sign that he couldn't believe what was happening to him. It was hurtful to see him rejecting it like that, as they were only trying to help. That's what people would do – try to help.

So I guess I realised there are similar qualities there, but the stubbornness of all of us in the family wanting to be together actually kept us sane. Because if we weren't like that, it wouldn't have worked for the family. I think I'm stubborn. I think Adam's got that same quality and it's double strength. Together we were able to navigate through this complex situation of children, friends and family all asking questions and trying to give unnecessary advice. Arguments were happening daily. Our parents did not understand how serious this situation was. Selfishness had got the better of them and the incomprehensible way they would talk to both of us sent me red with rage. Either they were pig ignorant or plain stupid. How on earth are we going to go back to normal? It was increasingly difficult to hold a conversation with Adam's parents. My Mum knew how bad things were, but could do little to help, as her own health was failing.

Every now and then, Adam and I would argue, and then I'd say, "I don't need you to be in here now." But he'd still come back, with coffee or something.

He'd say, "I'll just come back with something to eat."

I'd think, "Why are you being so nice? Why are you so nice to me? I have been so horrible to you and you're still being nice to me. I am the biggest bitch right now. I know."

It was very apparent, but Adam was just there, still there.

He said, "I'm not going anywhere."

I said, "Okay, I think I get that now, I get it."

There were also moments when we actually turned to each other. We actually acknowledged what had happened. And it was heartbreaking, tearful.

It was important that these moments happened, because we were so isolated. It was when he said to me, "It's like, you hate me. You hate me so much. Don't worry though, because I hate myself, because I can't even believe this is happening." This pain was unbearable. I wanted to leave because I could not stand the sadness, we both felt like we had failed as parents.

When we had that moment, it made it clear we had to work together. We needed it because we were both at such a low place. It was good to have that unity where we could actually acknowledge what was going on and be there for each other, because it was coming up to Christmas and it was the most desperate situation.

Adam was supportive. He was so shocked, but he was still there with compassion, love and care, which I clearly had avoided giving myself at that time. I didn't want anybody to touch me or anything. I just couldn't stand it. I'd just completely shut down. I was like Jenson. I think we were mirroring each other. So Adam just kept being supportive, like your loyal best friend. I guess that's Adam. He's always been like that. I just didn't see it. So, it was comforting for me, because I needed to feel loved. He's good at saying, "I'm going to do this because I think you need it, it's going to be a present." We helped each other by being kind and this made the situation for my daughter much better to handle. We got into a routine and created safety for the family. The children felt more relaxed with structure and routine.

I think that's when we started to repair ourselves. It wasn't easy, but it was a start to things slowly improving and Jenson benefited from it.

The best Christmas present

When you are touched with that unexpected kindness, it makes you feel hopeful, and it opens up your heart. Entertainers would come in and they didn't expect anything. "Oh, here you go Jenson, we heard you're in hospital."

Visitors were all very positive and uplifting, and they would play Jenson a tune on the guitar and then they'd give him his present. He started to interact more and it was almost like he was going to start talking. We'd been waiting for ages. It seemed like forever. Two months, just nothing.

We thought maybe we could take him out in a buggy and just let him see the Christmas lights outside, because in London, everything's lit up. It looks brilliant at Christmas. So we managed to get hold of this assistance buggy. It wasn't the best one in the world, but it would do. We got him in there, he was a bit floppy, so it took a little bit of co-ordinating to pop him in with the right supports. We took him out to the front of the hospital to see the lights. As we grew in confidence, we took him over to Ronald McDonald House for parts of the day. The fresh air felt amazing and gave Jenson something different to look at. He smiled with his eyes and tapped his Spiderman Slipper feet.

It was one of these days when we took him back over to Ronald McDonald House to have a coffee. I was feeling sorry for myself, so I got a big slice of lemon drizzle cake. I was sitting on the sofa eating it. Jenson was there sitting in his buggy and looking at my cake, and Mason was having his milk because he loves his food.

Then I heard a word, like Jenson had said something.

I said, "Well, what's the matter Jenson? I'm eating my piece of cake."

It took about 30 seconds or so, but he said the word "cake". It was the longest way of saying a word ever. I didn't know what to say. So then I just said, "Can you say phone?"

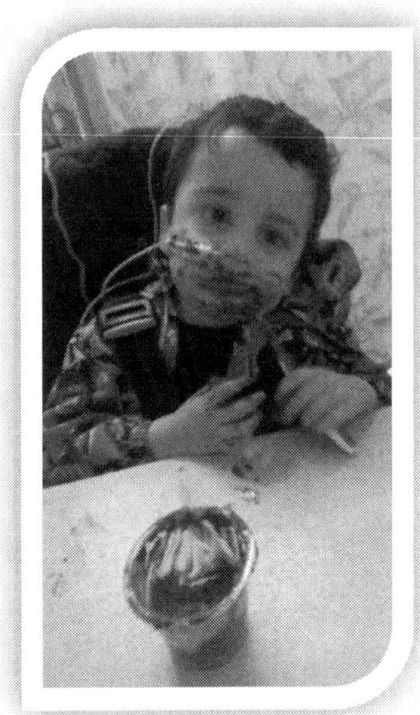

And then he said "phone". It was slow but, wow, he could actually communicate. So, there was miracle after miracle. They were small ones, but they made such a huge difference to him and how he was perceiving the world. I was delighted about this. I thought, well, if he can do that, he can tell people if he's in pain. This changes everything.

He just kept going for it. Communicating with his eyes before he could say the word. He wanted to recover; he was desperate to talk. He wanted to leave the hospital, so I just kept researching posterior fossa syndrome. I learnt that all the muscles affected really need to switch back on. Of course, it makes sense now that I'm reading it back again. That's why after surgery, everything switched off, and now he was rewiring and coming back 'on line'. So his speech was going to come back. He was starting to move – just twitches to begin with, as he learnt to co-ordinate his movements – but it seemed like everything would start to come back slowly.

This was monumental because we had so many issues with him. He couldn't eat, he couldn't do anything and everything that we were trying to get him to have nutritionally wasn't working. He had to have tubes. Basically, where his muscles weren't working, he wasn't digesting anything. So he was skeletal.

He went in a sizable, chunky toddler but he'd lost two or three kilos, so he was very weak.

My next port of call was to press for answers, to try and keep him motivated. I guess that's when I became more proactive. I had to get in there and ask the questions first before they came at me with all these other things, but I also had to be prepared for them to say 'no' to things that I was suggesting. Then I had this great moment of how I was going to approach his recovery. Not everyone was going to agree to it for sure. They disagreed with a lot of things to begin with. So I had to go back to the surgeon and just clarify exactly what the surgery had done, and be really clear about it and understand it, and confirm that the surgeon hadn't touched certain aspects of Jenson's brain, so there was no reason why he couldn't do things.

The surgeon said, "Yeah, sure, but you must work with your therapy team, because they'll have their own plans."

I said, "But, ultimately, what you've just said actually suits what I am about to do, what my plan is for his recovery."

He goes, "Yeah, I don't see why not."

So with that, I had to be courageous and confident that I was going to challenge people. I did that several times and my stubbornness was a good thing. It helped us get more calories into him. The more we gave him to eat the more energy he could use to recover his mobility skills. It was very simple, but he'd lost the simplicity of eating. I think I'd lost it too, because I'd stopped eating. Then I thought, "If he's not eating, he's not going to do be able to do half the stuff he wants to do."

So it became a mission and I guess from there that's how we got him going, how we got him talking. We got him doing lots of things by positive engagement in everyday activities. Eating together at lunch, playing games, getting ready for bed. Bath time was tricky, due to all the tubes connected to him, so a bed bath was used instead. We lay in bed with Jenson until he went off to sleep. Then we'd go off to Ronald McDonald House for the night.

Adam became even more Adam. He'd say things to me like, "Oh, you put a new t-shirt on today and you did your hair." We just started to take notice of ourselves a bit more, like we could actually see that there was a point where we could leave the hospital.

That was exciting. We weren't going to go home straightaway, because there was an enormous amount of work to do with Jenson and his recovery. But together, we stood a good chance of getting through this transition. Mason had grown up and had learned how to sit up and bottom shuffle across the floor. He was crawling and getting into mischief. He was happy if we were able to spend time playing and having fun. A typical little baby boy within an extraordinary situation. We moved around so many times in his first year it was a miracle how he just accepted it. I suppose it was an adventure for him. – it was a way we could move forward and plan for the future. We were in the present, but we knew if we took him home, we weren't going to be overwhelmed by this whole situation. We were going to be very much together as a family and working for it. So one problem at a time. That was the key point of how to get through this, one problem at a time. Because otherwise your head's in the sand. I just thought if I could do that, I'm doing something right.

I just chose a topic of the day. What do I want to achieve today? I want son to eat something. Okay. What else? Maybe say something. And what else? Oh, yeah. Move anything. When we accomplished these three simple goals, I was happy, because Jenson was listening, taking it all in. That's the power of a little person that you don't realise. They're taking in all this information that you're talking about in front of them.

Watch your (negative) language

So I became mindful. I started changing my language. It was very important to be more positive around Jenson, because it had a greater effect on him, rather than talking in a desperate way and in a sense that things were never going to be the same, that we were going to be changed forever, that he was not going to be able to do that anymore. He was listening to a whole lot of what we were saying and it's no wonder he wasn't participating.

If you're going to get depressed, that would surely depress you. So I changed the language I used with all the doctors and the therapists who would come around, and just tried to make it more upbeat. They all clocked the reasoning behind it. With that sort of twist on how you say things, it made him more able to just loosen up and try to do an exercise. Even if he got it wrong, he just kept trying to do it. That's still with us today. The team we go and see at the Royal Marsden Hospital are very mindful of how they talk around him, from the moment when we enter the room. If they say something and it's remotely negative, they correct themselves straightaway. They go, "No, we need to be motivating. No, no, that won't do."

I thought, "Wow, haven't we done well. We've kind of modelled our team around us to be the same bubble of positivity", and that encourages Jenson way more than anything.

Speaking up

With each procedure, there is always an element of risk against the potential benefit. A nasal gastric tube could always be inserted and positioned in the wrong place, resulting in a failure to get an aspirate from the stomach. As Jenson could not digest his food efficiently, he was often still trying to process the previous meal when it was time for the next meal. Careful observation allowed us to challenge the nursing team with regards to his feeds.

On one occasion, Jenson had his entire feed aspirated back out of his stomach. He was not digesting the feed and the nursing team failed to realise his enlarged tummy was a sign of the feed not being digested (this was a liquid formula that was fed via the nasal gastric tube using a machine to control the amount given). The problem was the calculation of energy expenditure and calories required did not add up. Jenson needed more calories, and it was then that I found the courage to speak up about the issue. Quite often, I would be left frustrated as I was not being listened to, so instead, I would use a visual demonstration to show the dietician or clinical nurse specialist how my son could be starving and very dehydrated.

Cue baby Mason and his milk bottles. By taking one of his bottles, I politely poured out a measure of what was supposed to be sufficient for Jenson's fluid intake for the entire day. It was shocking and by the look on the nurse's face, they were concerned and immediately set about providing more fluids via his tube. Sometimes, you need to be obvious with your concern as the medical team will assume that everything is stable and going well (I used to call this the automatic pilot mode). The danger of this assumption that all is well is that vital signs can be missed (Jenson's tummy was enlarged, indicating he was not digesting his fluid feed).

The intensive care ward was a busy place and quite often they simply did not have the time to just watch and wait. This was my job. When the ward sister checked the feed, she managed to aspirate the entire meal. The look of horror on her face said a lot to me, she was deeply sorry and wanted to put things right. I hated that things were frequently missed, but it happened.

Weaning

When Jenson was so hot and dehydrated, all I wanted to do was to give him a drink, but with all the protocols and nurses involved, he had to wait so long that he was barely managing to pass any urine. This was dangerous and I had to make them aware that his health was deteriorating because of it.

This part of the hospital stay had me incredibly frustrated, so I asked myself, "What are you going to do about it?" With that, I asked a series of questions while our surgeon was present. He confirmed what I knew all along. It was time to take back my responsibilities as a parent and bring my mothering experience to the hospital. What Jenson needed was to be weaned, just like Mason, who we were feeding tiny amounts of puree via a spoon and watching with keen curiosity as he made a swallowing movement. No signs of danger, phew, so we'd try another spoon, and it was the same for Jenson.

Jenson could eat without danger, so long as we gradually built him up from thick fluids to slightly solid food. As simple as this may seem, nutrition was a huge part of the recovery process, which I will mention later. If we could rebuild Jenson's ability to eat a regular diet, he would be able to heal his brain.

Being a bit of a nerd, I revisited some of the studies I did at university and recognised that some medical interventions would impact Jenson's ability to activate his digestive system. One aspect was the hyacin patch. This was a tiny patch applied behind the back of the ear to help absorb any excess saliva. The problem with this was that it gave Jenson a dry mouth and suppressed his appetite. When I showed the speech and language therapist that Jenson could indeed swallow without harm, I questioned the need for these patches and presented a logical argument to have them removed.

The change in Jenson's appetite was remarkable. He clearly wanted to eat and all we had to do was take our time getting the meals into his body. I really appreciated the expertise that surrounded us but had never considered my own skills with the same level of respect. I had an inspirational moment that I could trust myself. I got him to the hospital because there was something wrong, I stopped nurses giving Jenson morphine because something was wrong. Both instances relied on my intuition, a gut feeling. So why could I not trust myself now? I'd become too reliant on the medical team to produce solutions rather than trying to work through them myself. When I had this breakthrough, Jenson's progress began to take a turn for the better.

The finest brain fluid

If there was a time to turn to alcohol, it would have been in hospital while trying to cope with the relentless pressure of juggling the family. However, this part of our story is not about that. It is about the colour of cerebral spinal fluid (CSF for short). As eloquently described by our surgeon, the finest brain fluid should be as clear as gin (he mentioned this with a wry smile on his face).

Well, that was fascinating. As I looked down at Jenson's external drain, the colour was more like Appletiser, a deep orange. My immediate thoughts were that he had an infection, and after careful testing of this fluid and allowing cultures to grow in the lab (this takes a couple of days), I was right. All the medical team were on high alert as we were whisked back to intensive care. Jenson looked more awake than he had been in days, but he kept foaming at the mouth, like he was having a seizure. His heart rate was through the roof and he could not pass any urine. This, as it turns out, was a febrile seizure, which can happen when the brain gets infected. Time to bring out the Serious Infectious Diseases team. We were given an in-depth discussion about how clever bacteria and viruses can be, then Jenson was given a prescription for the strongest antibiotics available to treat it. Within a day or so, he was much livelier and his CSF colour was more like strong apple juice.

We were given the following spectrum of colours:

- Tizer / Iron Bru (dark orange with specs of blood)
- Dark apple juice (lighter orange with no blood)
- Apple juice like Mason's drink (almost translucent orange)
- Urine (straw-coloured, clear)
- Gin (clear as can be – infection gone)

I had never been so relieved to see clear fluid, it was the best Christmas present I could have hoped for. Jenson was getting better. Not only that, but he was also managing to move a little bit. He could tap his foot, raise his arms and say a couple of words. He was no longer a 'quadriplegic mute' as described by one of the registrars. Believe me, I scoured all 94 pages of his medical notes and could not believe my eyes when I read some of the things they were saying about my son. It hurt deeply but it made me feel a hundred percent better when I could turn around and use those exact words and say it to their faces. Jenson was far from being mute, he was only beginning to get his voice and movement back. Take that!! It was an example of hospital politics at its best and one of the many arguments I was willing to have to ensure my son's safety.

On one hand, they were saying he was a 'quadriplegic mute', but on the other, they were recommending that we take him home in our car for Christmas, even though he had next to no muscle tone, and to bring him back in the New Year. Hell no, this was not happening. Common sense had clearly left the building.

Christmas in hospital

As Christmas arrived, we were caught in a tricky situation. We dearly wanted to go home and celebrate with our family and friends, but we knew the care Jenson needed was best provided in hospital. We were not wanting to be killjoys, but the hospital had clearly forgotten about all the care components that we would have needed to have in place before we could even consider taking him home. There was clearly another policy in place that was taking precedence, which I will not go into, but it involved a certain bed crisis and the winter flu season.

After watching the nurses prepare Jenson for discharge, I had to disagree, it was something that made me experience a range of anger and pure frustration at how this healthcare system works. The way that it was sold to us as a family was that we could spend a lovely Christmas together and then come back as an outpatient in January to be discharged to Tadworth Court, otherwise known as The Children's Trust rehabilitation centre. In no way did they think about how this would work for us over this time frame. There was no consideration of Jenson's physical needs and the equipment he would need to use to just sit up. There was no mention of how we would get hold of a doctor urgently if we could not get an aspirate from his feeds. There was no mention of how he somehow could miss a week of his final antibiotics because it was the weekend before Christmas. Deep down I was seething, absolutely boiling over with anger. They were willing to let us take Jenson home in our car, in his car seat, with total disregard to the safety aspects of moving a child with little muscle tone.

"No way, no, no, no, no, no!" The nurses and Registrar turned round with surprise. I made it clear right then and there, Jenson was staying in hospital. I addressed them head on with regards to bed space and his own safety, to which they replied.

"We thought it would be nicer for Jenson, rather than staying in hospital."

"Really? How would it be nice for the family? Constantly on high alert because of the lack of specialist equipment and facilities?"

"Jenson is stable and has all his feeds prescribed, and you have received the training."

It felt like I was talking to a brick wall, so here I went again with my practical demonstration of how this would work, and It really did give them something to think about. There was no chance I would jeopardise his recovery by potentially making things worse for him at home, both psychologically and physically. He needed to stay in hospital. However, what they did mention was that there would be no therapists in over Christmas and that we would have to do all the rehabilitation ourselves until potentially into the New Year. Never one to shy away from a challenge, I gratefully received this information and set about creating a schedule to integrate his exercises using his various pieces of equipment. I knew that Adam would support me as we were working towards Jenson's recovery and helping him regain his motor skills.

So we continued his therapy in hospital over Christmas. I took over what the physio would do and started my own rehabilitation timetable. The equipment was not available, so we had to make up other ways to facilitate his movement by playing games and seeking out soft play materials. They had a sensory room, which helped, and a few mats. The rest was left down to us.

We spent Christmas together at Ronald McDonald House so that we could be together. It was sad not being at home, but it would have been even more unbearable to go back to a house frozen in time from when Jenson was last seen walking around without a care in the world. Everywhere would have been overwhelmed with memories of his life. All the bikes and cars he could no longer ride, the Lego he could not build. The kitchen where he would make pretend dinners.

It was heartbreaking. Every night in hospital, after Jenson would fall asleep, I would just cry. The nurses tried to calm me with kind words and lots of tea, but the reality was that our son we knew was gone and we missed him. The sudden effects of grief catch you off guard and I would be inconsolable.

We were trained to give Jenson his feeds and to find an aspirate, which allowed us to take him over to Ronald McDonald House for Christmas Day lunch. He loved being around his siblings but clearly felt sad that he could not play with all his toys.

He needed to move on to the next part of his life and that was coming with his discharge to The Children's Trust, a place where he could get the neuro rehabilitation and intensive care he needed without the confinement of a hospital bed. We were scared but ready to move. As we rode in the ambulance, Jenson was enjoying the fresh air of excitement of somewhere new for the next four months.

Takeaway: Creating a hospitable... hospital environment for your child

1) Become your child's advocate

   Trust that as a mother or father, you have that innate skill to communicate heart to heart with your children. Even if they cannot speak, hear or acknowledge you, they sense your presence. Whilst being faced with a bleak prognosis, if you feel that your child wants to fight it and get through this, be in their corner, help them voice their opinion and make sure that the doctors are aware of how your child is feeling. It is brilliant to have all this medical expertise, but what use is it if your child isn't mentally strong enough to cope?

2) Normalise things as much as possible

   To enable your child to come through this traumatic time, things need to be normalised. Business as usual. If they go to school or watch certain TV shows, it's good to maintain this in hospital. My son was so bored that I had to create a play area in our room. He still wanted to learn and be active, we just had to keep him safe. The hospital room would become Jenson's sanctuary of toy cars, gadgets and photos to remind him of home. Creating a calm, relaxing environment allowed him to rest as much as he needed.

Part II: Rehabilitation

Chapter 3: The Children's Trust Rehabilitation Centre, Tadworth

I want to go home

You want to get your son well, you're willing it. But it's you who's willing it. It's not him, because he's not feeling it today. He's had the wind taken out of his sails. He's just feeling down and you're trying to force him to go through this rehab and get to class now. And mentally he's not in even in the room. It's sad when you have that moment, when you really see he's just not with you. So you could have the best physio in the planet and can have all of the therapists together, but if he doesn't want it, they're not going to make any difference to his outcome. He doesn't want it enough.

That's when I changed. I thought, "Well, what does he want?" Because we've got everything here. "We're waiting for you, Jenson. What do you want?"

He said, "I want to go home." He didn't want to stay there. "Can you take me home, Mom?"

I didn't know what to do because it's quite a drive to get to this place. We'd come straight from the hospital to The Children's Trust Rehabilitation Centre in Tadworth and it's the only neuro rehabilitation place in the country that helps children. That's the key word, helps children. There are loads of places for adults, but only one that will help children in that detail in their initial phases of recovery. It's so sad because there should be a lot more spent on how to rehabilitate children who suffer with acquired brain injury. More investment would improve the outcome of their quality of life. Leading to more opportunities in the workplace or within sport, as Jenson enjoys swimming, he could change his physical weakness into one of his strengths.

When he said he wanted to go home, I was quite upset, because this was our opportunity to really get him moving properly and wanting his life back. But he just wanted to be at home. So I had a mutiny and I thought, "How do I make this work?" I saw a family come in that morning and she had drove her son in for the day. When we spoke, she mentioned about not staying at Tadworth but going home each day so it was like going to school rather than being away from home.

She said, "We don't stay here. We do all the classes on the timetable and then we go home at the end of the day."

Well, I didn't know you could do that. It would give me the opportunity to take him home, which is what he wanted. And with that change. My mind was made up. I would drive Jenson home everyday. It is because of this, his rehab really started taking off because he knew at the end of his day, he was going home. I hated the driving. I absolutely hated the driving. It meant going on the motorway, which would make me come out in a sweat. It was too much for me. At that time, I thought, "Oh, I can't do this kind of driving. It's unpredictable. People are driving at crazy speeds." But I made myself do it because I knew it was firing Jenson up to do what he needed to do. So I took my Calm Me inhaler with me to help relax my mind. It helped beyond words. The fears I had were not so much driving but if I hurt Jenson with any sudden brake or change in direction. Both of my babies were relying on me and the Seat Ibiza 1.4. had zero room after we had crammed all of the equipment we needed to take inside of it. My good friend Pierro would always offer a hand to collapse the assistance buggy and watch the kids whilst I figured this puzzle out each day.

I asked myself, "Kim, why are you doing this to yourself?" Then I thought, "I've got to because if I don't, this is going to continue." I had to really go there and get very uncomfortable and address all my own stuff with driving and the co-dependency of wanting someone else to do it for me.

"Ah, why can't you do it? Can you not drive me home?" And it's almost like a verbal slap in the face. "I can't." Then I thought, "Grow up. Let me take responsibility of myself and be grown up and do the driving, and just get him home and bring him back in every day." So after I had a talk with myself, again, that was life for the next two months. They were the best months there, because Jenson would come in ready to work, he was sharp, he was on it. My favourite tool to help me through this was my Calm Me inhaler. I created these for my clients, but the time had come to try it on myself. Especially with all the driving involved, my nerves needed to be in check.

Mason was tagging along with us and doing some of the classes. Even though he was 10 months old, he started to say "hello", things like that. The teacher took a double take.

She said, "He said, 'hello'. How old is he?"

I said, "10 months."

She was shocked. "He's talking already?"

He talks all the time. I didn't know how much of the therapy classes Mason was absorbing. Jenson was in class and Mason had the chance to listen. So it was early pre- school for Mason. By Mason Talking early, it helped Jenson to rediscover his own voice when he felt troubled.

Mason's very good with his alphabet and his numbers. And because they were good at the school teaching at such a pace that it was easy to understand, making it fun and singing about it, perhaps, Jenson and Mason both got educated to the same standard. Jenson loved having Mason around, as having his brother nearby was familiar. So when he was doing his classes, they were doing them together and the therapists didn't mind because they wanted him to engage in play, to do the activity.

We got so much more from Jenson because he wanted it. It was a different situation. He was suddenly making progress when they thought he had plateaued and that there wasn't going to be much more he could achieve. They'd thrown their hands up, "Oh, there's nothing more we can do with this. He doesn't want to show any interest in that." He then surprised everybody and started doing things. It was almost like he was listening to hear that he couldn't do it to then prove everyone wrong.

I thought, "Where does he get that from?" Then it occurred to me, "Oh no, it's me. Isn't it?" Because you have to get so uncomfortable first before you shift. He's doing the same, I thought, "Wow, that's incredible for him at his age, showing that level of stubbornness" and then to prove everyone wrong. And now I know his little secret.

I think he now knows that I know, and we can work at much deeper levels. So if I want to set him a certain task, I don't tell him, I pretend it's a game. I don't tell him that he has to do it in a certain way. He's excited to play the game, until he realises what I'm trying to do. Then I've got to change it slightly so that he continues doing it. But at the same time, he's going to hate me a little bit and that's fine. It's not personal. I'm just a therapist with a student.

In this moment, you're not mum and son. I'd have to put on a professional hat and go, "Right. We will finish this task. You are going to do some crawling and we're not going to give you all the support you need."

He'd say, "I hate you."

I'd say, "Okay, is that right? We'll go with that."

"Because I really hate you."

"Yeah?"

"Yeah."

"But I'm sure you do, keep describing it to me."

"I hate this. I hate you. I hate everything."

"Wow, you're saying it really passionately now."

As he's saying it, he's moving. Because he's so angry, he's moving his whole body with no support. He's moving his foot and his arm, and he's crawling across the floor. But he's screaming that he hates me.

I'm just looking at him amazed at that level of "I don't want to do this" that he's feeling, while he's actually doing it, but I can't let on. I'm just watching. I'm not rising to the bait and getting emotional and crying and indulging in a display of emotion to distract him, to prove him right. I'm just doing nothing. I'm still and he's going on and on and on.

"I hate this. I hate this place. I hate that one."

He's just moving. It's the best movement I've ever seen in ages. And I capture it. If you've got a phone or anything, it's good to get your child's progress on video. You copy it and you go, "Look, I've got a copy for life. This is what you've done." Then when he's at the end of his rant, I say, Jenson, "Can I just show you what you just did?"

He goes, "What? What have I done? I haven't done anything. I just told you I hated doing this silly exercise."

So I showed him the video of himself and he went, "Oh, my God!"

He was just looking at it saying, "That's me?"

I went, "Yes! You were just doing that."

He was shocked because for somebody who's had a brain injury and surgery, I guess you just don't know your capacity to do things again. So his shock at his progress was just a catalyst to then start doing other things, because he realised he could do it if he was engaged in it but not thinking about it.

So it's like the back door to treatment, doing it instinctively because you know that if your survival processes kick in, your body will do something to protect or to move you out of danger. So he couldn't control that. That was instinctive. So with my training with him, and it was just about mobilising certain parts of the body, it was about distracting him, so he wasn't thinking about trying to move his leg and his arm.

In time, it was more about, "Oh, have a look at these strawberries over here. Why don't you try and come over here and reach this one?" And he'd have to figure it out. I wasn't focused only on "Move your left hand, left leg...", because the more I focused on that, it wasn't happening, because he was overcompensating. It's almost like the balance in his head. He just couldn't get it right.

There are things we take for granted, for example, we correct ourselves if we're wobbling, but he couldn't do that. But if I just left it to open interpretation and just said, "Oh, why don't you reach this for me? Can you go and get that for me?" He would then go and get it because he was focused on the item and not how he was going to get there. And then I would be able to record or have Adam record what he'd done.

That's where the biggest shifts have been, because he's been unaware that he's actually done it. We've just been going, "Yes" in the background because we knew he could do it. It's sort of been about figuring out how our son learns, or how any kid learns, because you think you know best, but your way is not always the best. So me making him follow the instructions to the letter, "We must do this. We must do that", was building a big wall of resentment in him.

He didn't want to do it, because he'd been told to do it. But if I made it a request, he would openly help with that request. So it became a much better way of communicating with him to get the output. And for Jenson, it was massive, because it was the difference between being curled up in a ball, lying on the floor, doing nothing or actively trying to be part of something.

Frustration

"Sometimes, kids can scream in your face. They can lash out. They don't mean it. But when you're feeling sensitive as a parent, it hurts. It hurts a lot. They come at you. They're waving their arms in your face. They want to kick you and things like that.

It's their frustration, but you have to see past it. In all the sensitive moments we've had and the really painful ones where I was taking it personally, for my own sanity as a parent, I would always reflect on it an hour or so later and actually say to myself, "He didn't mean it."

You've got to think about what has happened to him, and ask why he would be frustrated, to then be able to break the cycle of you thinking you're not good enough, you're failing him and making yourself feel bad because you can't get him to the next level fast enough.

At times, I'd put pressure on myself by measuring his recovery by time and not going with the flow of how Jenson was progressing. Time pressure alters your perception of success. Slow growth does not mean it is worse than fast growth. However, when you compare your child with other children who are of the same age, it's self-sabotage and you have a feeling of failure, with yourself, with the school system and all the hoops you need to jump through. My mind was constantly fighting itself when it came to the comparison to other children. My Jenson was a warrior, but a wounded warrior, and even they need time to recover.

To them, there's no concept of time. We live by time, the school day, everything. We have to be up at a certain time in the morning. We have to do all these things before this time. Applying that same approach to recovery doesn't work. If you put a time frame on it, you're just going to be disappointed if your child doesn't reach it.

So Jenson was not walking and it had been a year later. Does that mean he's never going to walk again? You start feeling bad because it's not happening. You feel like it's never going to happen because you're waiting, and waiting, and waiting.

You don't know patience, so you have to learn it in this way because it's out of your hands. Every day, you're just wanting that sort of indication that it's going to happen. It's a spark of hope that he's going to do it. And it just doesn't arrive. It's like days go past and you think it's the same. He's not doing anything different. And then all of a sudden, at the end of the month or two months, there will be a change. He'll be doing something slightly different, but it's not as big as you expected.

It may be small to you, but to him, it's a massive thing. Our perceptions have to change to match our child's, because what I thought was a massive achievement was nowhere near what he thought was a massive achievement. To him, holding a cup without spilling, drinking without dribbling, was a massive achievement. Me wanting him to walk and then climb stairs wasn't in the same league of where he wanted to be. I was just goal setting. I needed to understand Jenson and I'd missed that. I was trying so hard to focus on his recovery, I misunderstood him or I just wasn't listening.

I could freely put my hands up and say, "Look, I wasn't matching my perceptions with his, and it's okay." But you can always start doing that. If you haven't been doing it and you're two months in, but you're starting to do it, well, that's good. You've noticed the difference. When you're totally ignorant and you never change, it could result in a child who's lost and just totally disconnected. And that's something I wasn't willing to experience.

So I was hard on myself in a self-development way to try to figure out what was going to help him. Good for him. I'm proud of him. I never used to say that either. I couldn't say proud without a negative attachment to it. I felt that was my problem, not his, because everything he does is sort of, "Look what I've done. I did it by myself." He gives himself a round of applause. He doesn't need me to do it. He's like, "Okay, but I'll do it because I'll make you proud of that." I can't believe that kid is just so smart.

Then he bowls me over because he can do it and it's right underneath my nose and I just go, "Huh? How long have you been this way? What have you done? Did you have something secret? Like a drink? I didn't know about that." I kind of lost that enthusiasm whilst being in the hospital up all hours. Things were happening right in front of me and I wasn't seeing it.

Repetition

Having worked with my daughter and her high-functioning autism, it was apparent that the repetition of certain tasks can help lower anxiety with regards to a social situation. I applied this theory to Jenson with regards to his innate signals for thirst, hunger, sleep and toileting. We did not know if his pituitary glands had altered throughout his recovery, but it was clear he didn't know how to self-regulate his needs. So I applied tools that would be used to help with autistic children, even though Jenson is not autistic. I applied the structure, routine and timing of each meal, comfort break, drink and sleep time. This was integrated into each day to allow for his body to respond. As time passed, Jenson became more aware of when he was supposed to be doing something. The repetition of keeping to time with each activity gave him the ability to notice when something was missing.

At school, Jenson became more independent through communicating my strategy with his Learning Support Assistant and SENCo (Special Educational Needs Co-ordinator). As with muscles, the brain needs some regularity with time. The more time you give to a particular movement, the better you become at mastering that skill. Muscles have the ability to remember movement, and only with repetition can a synapse be created to store this as a long-term memory, or what I would call an instinctive response. In other words, we are creating new neural pathways as the previous ones are gone. Everything Jenson will now learn will be like learning it for the first time with regards to his mobility. As you will appreciate it is a complex subject that requires a vast amount of research to enable the right types of exercise to do this job.

I am determined. I mean, I don't give up. I keep going. In the beginning, it was not always clear what Jenson wanted, but I wouldn't give up. "Well, that's not what it is, it's not that, it's not that, it's not that." And then you get to it. You think he's just tired and complaining, but then he's relieved because you found out what he wanted, because he didn't even know. I had to use visual cues to help Jenson understand what he was feeling and how it was connected to sleep, eating, drinking or being sick. His emotions were not intuitive to the action; however, I was intuitive to anticipate the right action with the mood he felt. This led to a breakthrough with his therapy team and how we would approach his sessions, by using a scale of 1-10 to gauge his tiredness or hunger level.

Reteaching him the basics of knowing when he is tired, when he needs to eat, drink and go to the toilet, because he doesn't have those innate functions, is very hard, because some days you think he's got it, but he hasn't. You think you've trained him to have those urges, because you've set up a routine and structure and repetition, but he doesn't come up and say to you what he needs. But recently, he has started to.

And you think, "The repetition has actually done something." By just being pigheadedly repetitive, following the same, groundhog day structure every day, for example, taking him to the toilet this time of the day, it's actually worked. Because it's got his brain to just go, "Yes, that's it. It's hunger. It's thirst, it's tiredness ." It's taken so long, but I'm really pleased with that. Recently, I thought, "He's doing it himself. He's actually doing it himself."

Body suits all round

I wanted to find something to support Jenson's core, so that he could be more mobile and get his independence back. I had looked at swimsuits but they weren't supportive enough. I moved onto wetsuits for surfing and jet skiing, and although the fabric they were made of seemed supportive, it was not reinforced with extra layers to help stabilise his hips and shoulders. Then I thought about getting a resistance band sewn in and Googled 'resistance band suits' on a whim. A company called DMO Orthotics appeared in the results.

DMO orthotics specialises in making hand-stitched suits to support people with low muscle tone and help them regain independent movement. They look a bit like a bodice, but they're made with resistance bands. The design is based on the belief that sensory feedback to the brain can help control the level of tension created by the muscles. It was exactly what I had visualised.

I called the company and spoke to a lady called Holly and explained Jenson's needs.

She asked me, "Do you think a body suit would be useful?"

I said, "That sounds good."

Then, I showed her a picture of what I was drawing and it was exactly like that.

I said, "You actually make them?"

They're like, "Yeah. We make them."

I went, "No way. That's exactly what I'm after. Because then, that would just keep him upright."

Suddenly, there were the people we needed. They're in the UK. They're based in Devon. They were nowhere to be seen, but then when you're looking for something, it's almost like somebody's going to show you that it exists. There it was. I was thinking, "You are kidding me." I was so happy. I was thinking, "I'll have one of them. I don't care how much it costs. I want one."

Before I knew it, we'd got a custom-made suit ready for Jenson. It was all stitched within a very small tolerance to keep Jenson upright and mobile, but also to strengthen him. So, it was making him work out. It was like me at the gym with my resistance band, except he's doing it in a suit. It's so intelligent. I love this piece of gear. He's had two now. It just does the job. I don't have to hold him now because the suit does it.

Getting Team Jenson on board

Obviously, I needed to get Team Jenson on board – the physio, the occupational therapist, the speech and language specialist.

They said, "All right. What's that all about?"

I had to tell them that I'd made some changes, because they don't like change. They've got their programme and it's good because they know what's happening, but then they think, "Oh no, mum's gone and got this. And now, what does that mean for us?"

I said, "It's going to help you. Hear me out."

Then, the physio said, "Yes, they used to do these suits a long time ago. But it was all to do with funding, so they stopped it. So, the kids no longer get a referral for one of these suits."

Well, Jenson comes along, he says, "I want one." Then, not only did he get one, seven other kids got one too, because he was referred. They have to get a certain number before they do a clinic.

He got the clinic. He got another seven kids a suit, because their parents thought, "Oh, we'll have that as well." It was brilliant.

Now, Jenson's just making up his own rules. I was really pleased for him and the others who will benefit from it because of him needing it.

I think, at the moment, the way he's working with that suit has changed the mechanics of how he holds himself. It's taught him good behaviours. Because there is a such a thing as recovering too fast from something and learning bad habits. That's something I wasn't willing to do with Jenson. The physio also agreed with me, but she's always suspicious of equipment. She wants him to work it out for himself.

I said, "But he will. This is just going to teach him what he needs to do and what he doesn't need to do. So, when he hasn't got the suit on, it's exposing everything he can't do. Then, he will adopt what that suit does because the body has tolerance. You put a jacket on every day and it feels a certain way. When you don't wear it anymore, you feel naked. It's a bit like that with your muscles."

If you don't push the muscles, they lose resistance. The muscles go back to what they know, why would they want to move? It's just so logical, but it gets missed. And why can't we communicate with compression? Because when we have something tight to our skin, it feels nice. It's like a blanket. So, it's comforting. That's exactly what the suit provides. It's like a reassurance that something is there holding him. And it's what we love in life, isn't it? It's like someone giving you a hug.

Whenever I propose new pieces of equipment to the physio team, they always say, "Why do you do that? Why do you want that?"

I say, "But this is the next step."

They say, "He's not ready for it."

I say, "I know that, but he needs inspiration and motivation to go to the next step."

If I don't get it in ahead of when he needs it, he won't be looking at it and eyeballing it in the corner of the room thinking, "I'm going to be using a stick soon because I won't need to use my walker." He's just getting his mindset ready now. He doesn't want to use his walker. He wants to be able to use a stick. Let's do this.

I bought that stick, or set of them, four months ago. They were saying, "Oh, it's too soon. You're pushing him."

I said, "I'm not pushing him. I'm just giving him that little message, a visual cue, here's what's next. And he's thinking how he's going to do it and then he's already getting there before you know it."

Time passes and he then gets to the next stage. So, I've realised my place. I need to be forward thinking to then get him to the next stage of his recovery. It's amazing because there's so much out there for kids, but it's not easy to find. I really wish it was easier for parents. Because when you leave hospital, you haven't got a clue. You haven't got anything. There's no timetable. There's nothing. No instructions about how you're going to do this rehab at home.

Takeaway: Preparing for transfer to a new facility

1) Preparing for discharge to the next facility is like a transition. It is best to embrace each location for what it is rather than comparing it to what it is not.

2) Rehabilitation can be like school, with a routine structure, which helps your child to regulate daily life and all the usual activities you would do.

3) Make notes either mentally or visually (ask for a map of the site) of where everything is. This helps to reduce anxiety and improve time management.

4) Having a timetable will also give you the times available to eat and drink in between classes, so you can keep energised.

5) Try and find toys and interests that your child loved before surgery. Sometimes this can keep them engaged in a certain exercise without them even knowing they are doing it. Cars, teddies, slime, action figures, pretend play kitchen, dress-up. Rule nothing out and keep it fun so you can laugh together. If you start the action first (pushing a car along the floor), they will try and copy (pushing it back to you). Keep a backpack full of these toys as they can help in physiotherapy and occupational therapy classes.

6) Make friends. Parents are often alone, and the lifestyle of constant appointments can leave you yearning for adult conversation. They understand how you feel and between you, you can just be yourself (crying, laughing, angry, whatever the emotion maybe). Some of my friends from this part of our journey are still around today.

Takeaway: What we learnt from the rehabilitation centre

1) Capture progress on video so your child can see how far they've come

2) Focus on the outcome, not how to get there – let your child figure it out. The biggest shifts come from when they're not aware that they're doing something

3) Don't put a time frame on achievements – it puts too much pressure on your child and makes them think they're failing

4) Match your perceptions with theirs – what is a massive achievement to them may not seem to be big to you

5) Repetition – builds muscle memory and synaptic connections

6) Being part of a group – encourages participation, inspires

7) Bad behaviour such as swearing is actually a good sign

8) Nutrition – the body and brain need wholesome food to repair and heal

Chapter 4: Chemo Diaries

On the home stretch – or so we thought

So when you're there, you're just in that moment, rather than thinking too far ahead, because that kind of then becomes a nemesis because you're daring to have hope. And if you think too far into the future, a curve ball comes and hits you in the face. It caught us off guard a lot. We were on the home stretch, we thought, when Jenson had finished from his rehabilitation at the Children's Trust.

We thought, okay, we're just going to focus on his rehab at home using the community therapists, get him mobilised, keep him moving towards his milestones. So that included all systems of the body – eating, drinking, sitting up, toileting, dressing, washing and brushing his teeth – and all the life skills of looking after himself. So much effort and attention was required as he was unco-ordinated and weak from surgery. Quite often he needed several pillows to prop himself into sitting position. His tummy had no strength, so holding a simple breath would have taken enormous effort. Talking and speech clarity had to be practised every day. For Jenson, this wasn't hard as he loved to talk, but the problem was that with his facial muscles being so unresponsive, many people would often find it difficult to understand him.

But with that said, and all this stress placed on the body to try and to do all this recovery, that tumour was growing in his head. We had no idea that that was happening. Because the same things came up. He wasn't being sick or showing those classic signs. He never had any seizures. The only little giveaway that things might not be so good was the fact that he wasn't progressing as much. His progress had slowed a bit and he'd plateaued. I remember the consultants saying to me that as long as you see progression, however small, if it's consistent, things are going well. I just had a feeling in the pit in my stomach that something was not right.

We went in for a scan in January 2019. Then we heard nothing. So normally, when you have no news, it's good news, because it means that they haven't got much to say, but this was different. We got it so wrong with that assumption. Because after they did that scan, and then received the results, they had a multidisciplinary team meeting. In those two weeks, they were formulating a plan to help him. Then when we went in for the check-up with the neurosurgeon, we were completely floored with what he was coming out with. I mean, his face wasn't happy, but he was glad to see Jenson. He was very businesslike, concerned. So I knew immediately when I went in that there was something that was going to happen. My body just went into that mode of just, well, okay, let's just deal with it and put this worry to one side, and just sit there and listen to what happens.

But the feeling of something not being quite right was just as uncomfortable, giving me cramp-like spasms in the pit of my gut. I sat there, he showed me the scan, and then we both just looked at it, shocked. We just couldn't believe it. We were thinking, are you fucking serious? After all this, it's back again? And it's growing? It was unbelievable. You think you've already been through enough, and then you hear these words coming out of the surgeon's mouth, and you can't hear them properly. They're muffled, maybe like you've got headphones on. You just can't hear what he's saying. You know he's saying that chemotherapy is his best shot, but you can't take it in anymore. It's just all in slow motion and you're in total disbelief. You just don't want to hear it. That's probably why what they were saying didn't come across clearly.

Then like a wave, like someone slaps you in the face, you wake up. Then you're hearing all this information and it's clear again. The surgeon is telling you what they need to do. They are unable to do surgery. Look what happened last time, it's too dangerous. So we have to do a referral to the Royal Marsden for chemotherapy. We don't know how long it will be for. It may be weekly. It may be monthly. There we go again, the uncertainty. We have no idea, no time, no objective, no idea what is going to happen.

But hearing the word chemotherapy is never a good thing, because you know what that medicine does to people. It's like nuclear medicine, it just totally annihilates your immune system to then allow you to make a new one. And it's happening to a very small little boy who's already struggling because he's trying to overcome a huge trauma to his brain from surgery.

You're trying to think of ways to make this come across well to him, because he's in the room and he's not deaf. He can hear everything and what that would mean to him. That shock and that way your body reacts is protective, because not only do you need to receive that information, which you do, even though you're in an emotional state of overwhelm, but you're in a position where you've got to relay that in a positive way to your child. Otherwise, they're not going to be able to react very well either.

I think from Jenson's perspective, he just wanted to know what had happened. There were some things he was feeling that he couldn't describe. He couldn't articulate them, because he couldn't talk very well to tell me. Then when we got that picture and it's really clear to you what's happened, you've then got the answer and it's not what you want. It's a worst-case scenario.

You'd accept it better if it was just a glitch in something, maybe he needed more vitamins or minerals or something, but this was how we didn't want it to happen. Sitting there 18 months after all that had happened to us, this wave of our biggest fear was coming at us again, with the possibility of losing our son because of how strong this medicine is and what it does to the body. I couldn't comprehend that this was going to happen. We had so little time to get ready, because they wanted to get started straightaway.

We got home and I was just in this state of shock, knowing that our whole life was going to be turned upside down again and not knowing how long that was going to be for. We had an appointment at the Royal Marsden and I sat there with a consultant, and it was like starting all over again, a brand new consultant, a new hospital, the need to tell her all Jenson's history. They'd had a meeting, but they still needed lots of information.

So luckily, with all the notes I'd taken, I was prepared, and I was able to reel off dates, times, procedures with accuracy. But at the same time, she had to tell me that they wanted to start chemotherapy that following week. The course was going to be 72 weeks. Okay. It's not a small length of time. Our whole life was going to be different for 72 weeks.I wasn't prepared to let her start the chemo straightaway. That sounds bad, calculating, but it was simply because I needed to go away and have a week where I could plan what was going to happen during those 72 weeks, because there would be so much going on. With the way it was going to be done, and how she was talking about it, she was very optimistic. You would be, because you're the consultant, you know how these things work. You've treated many children. You know the outcome, the tumour, and it all makes sense. But to a parent, it makes no sense. You're scared beyond belief and you need to get a handle on this.

So I asked her for more time.

She said, "I suppose we can allow another week. Then we'll have to start."

I knew I needed that time. And so did Jenson. As a family, we needed to figure out how this was going to work. So, that week, I've never been so exhausted in all my life. I made sure we had a break and went somewhere as a family. It was before Covid hit, so you could just go anywhere and not be restricted.

We didn't leave the country. We stayed in the UK because we needed to be near a neuro surgical unit, but we spent a lot of family time together, making sure Sophia was happy and Mason could be his usual playful self. Just keeping everything the same, having fun together, and being aware of what was coming up but just enjoying every moment. We knew things were going to change, but we didn't know how they were going to change or if Jenson was going to be the same after another major change in his life.

So while we were having our holiday, I was also researching, till my eyeballs felt dry and I literally could no longer read another word. Using resources like Pub Med, which I had used at university, I researched about the particular therapy that was being presented to us for Jenson: what the consultant was going to do, the drug, the success rate, everything that could become a risk factor, what would help. Then out of nowhere my phone stopped working. The screen was blank, there was nothing I could do to reload it, it completely shut down. As exhaustion hit me like a huge wave, my body felt the same. I had shivers, a horrible onset of flu that stopped me in my tracks. Maybe this was a sign to rest and surrender to what would happen next. So having read what seemed like a dissertation on Vinblastine chemotherapy, I collapsed into a deep sleep.

All these intermittent insomnia episodes, and this sort of absorption of knowledge, just culminated in this huge sleep and me forgetting all my passwords. So when I woke up, I couldn't get into my phone. I went to my laptop. I couldn't get into my laptop. I couldn't remember any of the codes, because I was so stressed and overwhelmed with all this planning I had to do. They'd just escaped in my head. It was like starting afresh, I had to reset everything. I was so frustrated with myself because I know I should remember such things.

But when you are in a high state of emotion and dealing with a terrible bout of flu, you can't remember anything. The more I tried, the worse it got, I was locked out of everything. So I had to spend a day resetting all my technology so that I could communicate with the consultants and know what was coming up. When I got that sorted out, we were at the end of the week and the doctor was looking forward to seeing us on the Tuesday.

I took this research paper with me, in my bag. It was a just-in-case bag, a Mary Poppins bag. It had everything in it. Nappies, tissues, toys to distract, snacks, notebook, pens and a lovely tin of home-made calm-me balm. This bag was my portable office/Mummy bag. It had everything that I might need for Jenson. This bag is just brilliant, it's got everything.

We had all the kids with us because they couldn't be anywhere else as it was half term and they weren't at school. So we had to take it in turns, who goes in the hospital, who doesn't. Adam would be in the car waiting with Mason and Sophia, and I would be in the hospital with Jenson.

Being on the same page

We just needed to know what was best. We went in and the consultant came out, and she told me about the research paper she was basing her proposed treatment on. It was the same one I'd got in my bag. I felt a huge relief, because out of all the papers, and there are loads of research papers, she went with the same one I had.

I felt reassured that she was the right person for the job, because there was a connection. It made me feel even more reassured that she would be one of these consultants who would see a job through and who would pay overwhelming attention to detail. She picked up on everything and wanted to work with us. So it made me drop my defensive barrier, so I could communicate better. She was just as shocked as I was that I had the same paper, because at first, she didn't believe me.

I said, "I've got it." I picked it up and showed it to her.

She said, "Wow."

I said, "I like to do my research."

She said, "Well, of course, parents would do that."

I then asked my other question, because I didn't feel stupid anymore. Never ever feel stupid, whatever your question is, because there could be 10 other people who have asked the same question. So I asked about simple things like, how is this going to operate on a weekly basis? And if we do this, what do we need to do to make it safe for Jenson? Because you know, he could get all these infections. We were going to be in hospital a lot. She had answers to everything, but she didn't ever guarantee anything, because she knew she couldn't do that. That's what I expected, but what I did get from her was that I was already doing the right things instinctively.

I just said to her, "Is it possible that we could have this treatment at our local hospital for the following weeks, so that we can save on journey time as a family.

She said, "Sure, we can transfer that."

Sometimes you never know, and you carry on worrying that it's never going to work. But you've got to ask the question.

So with my research and keeping my journal and making notes of who I was dealing with, I was able to liaise with the local hospital near where we live, as a well as with the Royal Marsden.

This was another brilliant sign that it was going to work a lot better in the long term than I'd originally imagined, because we could then work around a closer hospital. School runs, picking up the little one, doing things like your work when you can, it was going to be achievable. We could work around that. If we'd had to have gone somewhere miles away, say an hour-and-10-minute trip each way, we would have been knocking out a couple of days of our week and we didn't know how Jenson was going to feel after each session. So it was vital that we could take him for treatment at a local hospital near us. That was another sign that things were going to move in the right direction.

Not every request could be met, but then I expected that. Those 72 weeks were going to be very difficult because we had to factor in school and everyday life. Jenson was still recovering his skills. So there was the multi-therapeutic discipline of the physio and the occupational therapist, the speech and language therapist, the ophthalmologist, and the round trip to all these appointments, plus the chemotherapy on top.

When I had to relay this information to each one of these therapists, they were shocked, because it's a massive blow to the collective who are trying to help him get better and become independent. They wanted to figure out the best way to keep going. I said to them that we needed to continue as usual and do the normal activities, irrespective of this treatment, so that Jenson could keep his routine.

All we were doing was adding an extra bit in, which he'd get used to. For him it was vital, because he had to keep recovering his skills, which he continues to do now. Consistency was also very important, picking the same day every week, which the doctors and nurses loved actually, because it made it easier as they knew when he was coming in.

The resilience of children

Every Tuesday was bloods day. "Okay, Jenson, let's get you ready for bloods. You know you love that."

We used every distraction technique going, every book we could find that he liked reading. We'd get it ready, squidgy toy, stress ball, whatever he needed, and the nurses would do their best. It could be that there was needle precision and they could get the blood. Or it could be that they couldn't get the needle in. Then there could be a bit of a problem. There'd be a wrestling match, and they'd get just a little bit of blood, but they still managed to get the job done.

It's just very difficult with children who have to go through that consistently every week, because their body doesn't want to do it after a while. It's sort of like someone who has diabetes and has to inject, eventually the scar sites get very sensitive. If you get bloods taken in the same place, the area gets very sensitive.

So Jenson had something like a little port. I liked to think of it like a drum with a skin on it. Every time he had to have blood taken, it was like having a poke in that same bit of skin. By the end of it, it looked like a pin cushion. There were so many little holes in that bit of skin. It was unreal. The body is marvelous. It will take so much stress and trauma. It will just keep going, because it knows that its ultimate objective is to get better. With Jenson, that's exactly what he did, he did what was expected of him every single week.

He didn't cry. He didn't make a huge fuss. Yes, there was this little bit of wrestling to try and get him to understand why this was happening. And then he would understand that it was going to make him feel better. When you have to keep repeating that message every week, you are training the brain. I think that's when we started to realise that the power of what we were saying to him had an effect on how he tolerated it.

All the surgeons and doctors thought he managed very well. He was such a good boy. So brave. He just carried on doing what he needed to do. You couldn't have asked any more of somebody, even if they were an adult. That particular quality of Jenson's is just so admirable. I was just in awe of that little person, because of what he'd put up with and all the stuff he had to continuously put himself through. And he did it without a fuss. I just sat there going, why can't I do that? What's wrong with me? Maybe I'm weaker than this little person. I've underestimated him massively.

You think that because they're small, they wouldn't possibly cope with it. The actual fact is it's you who can't cope with it, and they're turning around reassuring you. There's nothing to be afraid of. When they turn around with their arms open to you, and they say that, it just makes you feel really upset and angry at yourself, because how could you not be like that too? Just be fearless and step into that courage like they're doing, so that you can be strong for them. In that sense, we had to take courage from him, because at that point, I don't think we had that much. We were empty and just feeling hopeless because there was such a long journey ahead.

Yet, he had this way about him, this half grin, like he knew what he was doing, and we let him go with that. His sense of humour actually helped us, the little jokes he would make and the way he carried himself helped us, lifted us up, because we just didn't know how to react.

When you see your child having to have all this medicine put into them and the way they get the needles ready, you're just thinking, oh my God, they're going to put all this into him. And you're trying to keep him distracted. Your body's just going, wow, what is this? You have to do this every week. When you're driving the car to the hospital and you know what's coming up, everything becomes surreal. It's like you don't have another life, this is your life. And what you had before is gone.

So it's just this cycle, and it's repetitive. Like it was in the hospital, except this time it's repetitive with the treatment. Our fear was that if he went into hospital so many times, he could catch a different infection. There was a high infectious risk. He was having chemo and he was immunosuppressed.

He'd likely pick up the slightest cold or bug going around, especially if he went to school. That was frightening because it would take him so much longer to get over. What do you do? We could sit there and just stop doing everything we used to do and just live in this bubble between home and hospital or we could actually keep going with our life. I chose the latter option, to keep going with our life, because I personally needed to connect with other people.

It was not natural to me and it wasn't natural to Jenson. He was getting very down and depressed about not seeing anybody. So in this madness, I asked the consultant if he could go to preschool to see his friends?

She said, "Yes, it's okay. You can do it."

When I got the go ahead, it just shone a bit of light on the situation, because we weren't going to know whether chemo was going to work until Jenson had a scan three or four months later – that's how long you have to wait.

Back to preschool

So I approached the preschool and, at first, they were very, very apprehensive of having Jenson in there. After I told them certain ways to handle him, how that could work, and the physio had a word and the team I knew had a plan, they said, "Well, let's try it for a couple of sessions a week."

Jenson attended for just two hours, because he was unable to do more than that. It was the best medicine for him. Obviously, I was scared to let him go into the arms of his previous key person, because Karen was also in shock over who he was, from where he was, and that really got to her.

But Karen got her head around it. She's a very strong-minded lady and she was immensely popular with Jenson and he absolutely loved her. So when he knew that he was going to see Karen, I was thinking, he loves Karen, this is good. The lights went on and he started to sort of brighten up a bit when they would have a couple of hours together for two sessions a week. There wasn't an awful lot he could do, but he was observing all the other kids around him in a small environment, because they had low numbers, and it was good for him because then he got a bit more attention, a bit more one on one, which was exactly what he needed.

And with that, he responded well to the treatment, as he was not focused on it. He had other things going on in his life. Jenson was just looking around at the other kids and getting on with playing and chatting to his friends. Playing cars, dressing up and participating in stories, listening and enjoying the atmosphere of the other kids. He missed this quality time and I did not realise how important it would be for his social awareness of others his own age. Going back into something that he used to do and to have all that joy and happiness around him, and watching the other kids bouncing ideas off of each other and just being mirrors to one another was just what he needed.

It was the catalyst to spark something in Jenson to improve in himself mentally. With each week that went past, he just didn't notice the chemo. It was becoming part of his weekly routine. And the weeks were clocking up. Then it was time for the three-month scan. With that scan and with all the hard work and the nutrition we'd put into him, making sure we were helping him, there was a reduction. (I had studied the nutrition of other brain tumour survivors and how they changed their diet to minimise the growth of their tumours. Eliminating sugar and reducing carbohydrates were some strategies I had implemented. The consultant couldn't believe it either. She was just amazed. She had this grin on her face. She was delighted. We were over the moon with that because we just needed that bit of good news, because with all our efforts, the planning, what we're trying to do with him, we just needed to know we were on the right track and that we were doing things properly.

So that was like us getting the go ahead with our plan, "Well done, keep going. You're doing everything right." But it was very stressful to keep doing everything right, because naturally you want to rebel against such a rigid routine, the sameness of every week. Inside, I was fighting it. I wanted to break out of this sameness to do something spontaneous, and that little gremlin of spontaneity was just eating away at me all the time. I wanted to go and see my friends, have the family round to our house, but I knew that I couldn't do it because we needed to isolate for Jenson's sake. The risk of someone coming in who had a cold or had some other kind of illness like chicken pox, shingles, you name it, was a very, very serious risk and that risk just wasn't worth taking.

Celebrating the end of chemo

Then when Jenson had his last chemotherapy treatment during lockdown, in July, it was like having a party. I told the football club where I volunteered part-time, and they were all happy and excited, and shouting, "This is great news." And the running club I became part of was also supportive, they were constantly championing him to be better. These communities helped our family to reconnect with the outside world of chemotherapy.

It's something you cannot describe, but your good news becomes their good news like a cascade of positivity. Both clubs wanted Jenson to be well again. Having communities like this was monumental to us as a family. We finally felt we had people in our corner, championing our success but giving us the strength to continue our pursuit of recovery. Jenson has been a source of inspiration to many and, for me, observing his highs and lows, has given me the job of a guide. I seek the resources we could use and Jenson rises to the challenge of using them.

We thought it was amazing that they weren't going to do anymore chemo and he would just be able to be himself without having any further treatment.

When you're told that, a big weight lifts, straightaway. That's the joy of the situation. You endure so much, and that 72 weeks was like a never-ending battle week to week, with juggling the symptoms of chemotherapy, the sickness, the nausea, the tiredness, the inability to move properly. His eyes were doing some strange things that were all related to the medication.

We were still managing to get him to do some things like reading and participating. It was incredible because it had been a long time. I don't think I'll ever forget that. It was the four-year anniversary of it all. We had some tears and Jenson watched himself on some videos, from the beginning, when Mason was a little baby lying on his hospital bed annoying him. Jenson was laughing, as he thought it was funny. Looking at the video now, Jenson was like, "Oh, he was only playing, wasn't he? And I really didn't want him there."

I said, "So did you see how you were trying to push him off?"

He was just having a little laugh, but at the same time, he was watching his progress, because of where he was. It made something click in him, that he was doing such a great job. It is very difficult what he's trying to achieve, and I just wanted him to see where he'd come from, because I think it got to a point where he couldn't see that he was making any progress.

But he was, all the time. When he was in school, naturally, he felt like he was out of place, because everyone was doing so much more, but he was at school, and when he was there, he could learn whatever he wanted to learn.

I told him, "Don't worry about not being enough, because we all have everything we need. If you want to learn more, we will find a way, it's not about being hopeless anymore."

That's what I enjoyed saying to him the most, "Whatever happens, you're going to be fine."

He was listening to that and it was soothing, because he was worrying. You could just see him thinking, "I don't really want to go in school. I hate it."

There was so much expectation on his shoulders to do things. Every specialist who came in wanted him to do all these different tests. They're not easy to do either, because you need to focus and concentrate.

I think he just thought, "I don't want to do it anymore. I just want to play."

Seeing himself on video, he just realised, "Wow, I'm doing so much more than I used to."

I said, "Of course you are, and you're taller, and you're bigger, and your brother's bigger too."

Chapter 5: Covid Comes to Town

Shutdown

We were getting into our routine, Jenson was getting better, and we were enjoying a little bit of calm. Then Covid came into town. Hang on a minute. What is this? I pick it up on TV. Some sort of virus thing? I was like, well let's not think about it too much. But then people were getting ill and, come January, there was talk of this coronavirus. Not once did we think that this could have possibly been something that might have been round and already affecting us, but it seemed like it was around a lot longer before they talked about it on TV.

Even so, we had no idea that the whole of the country was going to shut down. It was the strangest concept that could ever happen. Then, you feel a wave of dread. It's the day when Jenson's school says, do you think your son should be in school because of these increasing Covid cases? And on the same day, the hospital says to not bring him in. But he'd already been in last month. He'd already been in so many times, and we were then swept up into isolation. So we couldn't go anywhere. So I'd found my freedom. I was doing this, doing that and it was all taking shape and then, wow. Everything stopped again. You'd think we'd have been used to these shocks by now, but it still took us by surprise, because now we had our son home 24 hours a day again.

We had to care for him and educate him. But not only that, the lockdown was extensive. So now we had Mason, who's into everything and up to no good, because he's a toddler and that's what they do. And we had Sophia, who's actually home as well. Curriculum, school, how do we do this?

Then Adam said, "I can't go to work because Jenson needs to be isolating."

I said, "Exactly. So you can't go in either."

The money situation. What are we going to do? The government came through with all these furlough schemes. It must have been awful for everybody, but I just felt like we were hit by a bus again, because we'd only just got to the point where we were feeling cautiously optimistic, getting on top of things again, and then it was just dashed. We couldn't go out. What were we going to do? We had to do everything at home.

We had a good neighbour at the time, who had a cross training machine he never used. It was gathering dust in his garage.

He said, "Do you want that?"

I said, "I'll take it."

We set it up outside with these little mini weights from the supermarket, so that Jenson could lift them up, proper Rocky style, doing his repetitions. One of our friends from the local football club offered us this machine that he could sit on that simulates horse riding.

She kindly dropped it off because we couldn't go anywhere. It's a really cool piece of equipment and it would do what horse riding would have done for him if he'd been able to go, because he used to go every Friday, but when Covid arrived, everything closed. So our outdoor gym was looking all right. It was looking good for Jenson's physical education. It's just that we needed help with everything else, like maths, phonics. You have no idea how much the school does until you have to do it all yourself, and it's a lot. We were joking, "You fit all this in a school day? How do you do that?" Then you've got to make lunch. I was like, how many hours do you need for school, because I was thinking, "I'm going to change the school day to suit what we can actually do."

Being creative, I just thought, well, you don't tend to do music and drama a lot at school. Let's do it at home. So I got them all doing a bit of music and dance, which then gave me a chance to tidy and then get lunch while they were occupied. Then we'd all have a good go at maths. Obviously, Sophia needed to have a different level of maths than Jenson. So I downloaded some apps onto the computer and that helped massively, because we were able to track her progress. She could just log in and do her hour. It was like a complex Rubik's cube, because we didn't know what was going to happen with this COVID situation. So I just took a day at a time.

We still had to go into hospital, which was even more scary because of Covid. They were not going to come out to us and administer Jenson's chemotherapy, because legally and for insurance purposes, there was lots of red tape around this. They weren't going to budge. Even though it would've been the best solution, we had to live with the fear of taking him into hospital every week during the pandemic, knowing full well that he could pick Covid up at any time. So with that, we just had to manage our mental mindset. Positive reinforcement, breathing deeply and listening to the consultants for updates.

Making home school fun

But what I did try, and continue to do, is to make learning fun. I'd just come up with random stories and characters that the kids could make. One day, I said, "Make your own character, and you can tell me everything about them." Then I took this little bit of paper and made a drawing with speech bubbles. Jenson laughed his head off, because it was the most unusual character I'd ever seen in my life.

He said, "It's an alien."

I would second that, it did look like an alien, but he had a lot of personality and he wore a hat. He had very long legs and was capable of superhuman skills.

Jenson said, "Regeneration."

I said, "Is that what you're doing Jenson? Are you regenerating yourself?"

He said, "Yes, Mom, that's exactly what I'm doing. I am a ninja."

I said, "Okay, right, that's interesting. So what we can do with that in an English phonics way is that we can write about that."

So he gave me all the ideas and I'd just read them back to him. He found a lot of pleasure out of that. When we were trying to look at words, he would come up with silly words and then rhyme them. So I knew that there was a skill there. He was able to rhyme words to make sense of them, and he was remembering them. So we were doing quite a lot of healing together, because he was catching up with some schoolwork, because it was one to one again, at home. Also, he was keeping his appointments at the hospital.

So with that, eventually his school contacted me to say they had a place, but it wasn't his regular school, because it was for the children of key workers, and children who had educational healthcare plans, which Jenson had, so he was entitled to a place.

Part of me didn't want him to go there, because there was a risk. But I knew from previous experience, when he went to a school, he felt a lot better, because he was around other children his own age.

Takeaway: Creating a rehabilitation programme at home

With lockdown came the daunting task of creating exercises that Jenson could do at home and that were beneficial but not harmful to certain systems in his body. These are the key things I became aware of:

1) **Time**: Make sessions short, around 20 minutes maximum or what your child can tolerate. Believe me, if I used cars and Paw Patrol, which were Jenson's favourite things, he would surpass this time but still retain a cheerful outlook.

2) **Variety**: Just because your child has experienced a brain trauma does not mean that they cannot enjoy looking and engaging in new things. Strong, big-type visuals were great to get Jenson's attention and help him learn his numbers and the letters of the alphabet. Researching his eye condition and what he needed was key to developing this and using Ronald McDonald House for various toys which we would clean and return added variety to his own toys.

3) **Observation and patience**: At first, we thought that Jenson could not talk. It took a long time to gauge his response, but I persevered and realised that he could respond verbally. He took around one and a half minutes to answer a question. This was progress, so be patient as much as possible. Each time you invite your child to answer your questions, they will get a little quicker. It takes practice to flex these vocal cords to get stronger and build that connection from the brain to the muscles.

4) **Engage all the senses:** Make play tactile and use the sense of smell to stimulate memories that remind your child of happy times, Mummy or Daddy, or siblings. This can be such a comfort when you are so far away from home. Physical

contact like massage will promote circulation and help the sensory feedback to the brain. Try the feet first then work up to the legs and arms, as laying in a hospital bed all day can make the muscles stiff and sore. So, if you do a little massage before your physical therapy, it will warm the limbs up before a workout.

5) **Tone of voice**: When my son could not see very well, I made my voice a source of comfort. By telling him what I was doing, where everything was and how we were going to work that day, he could let me know by his facial reactions (even with facial palsy) if he was happy or in pain. Hearing became the strongest sense and even when we work out together today, he still listens carefully. It is true when they say if you are too emotional, you cannot be listening. If temper tantrums flare, then wait until things calm down, but always explain to your child why you want them to do something. Make eye contact, so you know you have their attention. To them, it will mean that you are being open and honest, creating a safe space.

6) **Encouragement**: You would want the same encouragement if someone wanted to make you do exercise and you were not in

the mood or felt that you could not do it. Trust is a huge part of taking those next steps and your child will need to feel that they can trust themselves before doing an exercise. Reaffirming a positive comment or statement will help them. "I've got you", "I will be right here" or "You are safe, you can do this."

Chapter 6: Relentless Pressure to Improve

The teachers wanted to point out where Jenson needed to improve, but when you keep doing that to a child, they start to feel like they're not enough, that they're never good enough. It's massively important to have a conversation with the school and point out to them that maybe they could do things a bit differently and change their language so that it becomes more positive and motivational. You'd be surprised that even teachers don't always use motivational language, and then they wonder why kids don't want to go to school or want to be in their class.

They would say to me, "Well, Jenson filled this form out and he said he really liked it here, and he's excited."

And I'd say, "Which part of the form do you think he was being honest with? Or do you think he was just saying something you wanted to hear? Maybe he didn't want to upset you. If you'd ask him a real question, you would get a different answer."

They were surprised in our meeting, as they thought he was happy and enjoying himself.

I said, "No, some days he really hates it, he doesn't want to go out the door. And I have to have a conversation with him every morning to put him in a good mindset to get him there."

They were surprised and said, "That's not what he says on the form."

I said, "But that's what you're always about, isn't it? Forms, ticking boxes. Are you a square? Are you a circle or a triangle? Well, no, he's none of these things. Emotionally, he can be a mess, and you're not looking at that, and you are wanting him to conform to a certain standard, instead of just looking at him and where he is, and that's where it's been missed."

They didn't have an answer for that. I said, "You're not looking at his emotional wellbeing. You're drilling in phonics and wanting to bring him up so that he's keeping in touch with the year. But you've lost him, because as long as he is in this emotional turmoil of not wanting to be there, frustrated and angry, he's not going to be intellectually working at his best."

Then the penny dropped with the teacher. She said, "Yeah, of course, then that would explain why he's frustrated and he doesn't do what I ask him to do."

I said, "Well, no, because if you wake up and you've had a bad night, and you've got a teacher who insists that you must do this, you just rebel. That's just him telling you, 'I don't want to do it, I'm fed up with you, and for once it's not perfect'." But you're trying to smooth over all the issues and get some perfection, which doesn't exist.

"Jenson just needs to work from day to day and keep motivated, so that he's still there at the end of the week, because if you are in and out of a depressive state, because you don't feel you're ever good enough, you're in this well of 'I'm never going to be good enough, so why should I bother?'"

She said, "Well, what's it like at home then?"

I said, "Well naturally, at home, you have to distract that thought process. So we just bring fun and a lot of creativity, and we just tell him to spend time being himself."

What does that mean? Jenson likes Lego. He likes to make junk models out of cereal boxes and toilet rolls, with lots of glitter, stick bottle tops on things to make cards. He has oodles of time, because we give him plenty of time, and that makes him happy.

When he goes to school, it's all structured and very regimented, which makes him unhappy. So what we have to do is find a balance.

I hope that this message has actually gone in, because maybe now they will realise that all these tests they're trying to get him to do have got him to a point where he just doesn't want to do them anymore.

No more tests, because they're not bringing out any new results. In fact, the test might not even give a true result of what he is capable of, because he's just so damn fed up with them.

He's like, "I'm just going to say whatever", and then they're going to mark that down as that's him. And you know two days later that isn't him, because he would answer it a different way. So it is just so ambiguous. But I feel for him, as this is a lot to ask every day, in a mainstream school. So at home, we allow him that time to chill out, as it's very important.

I feel for the school also. That meeting at school about Jenson made me look at the whole picture and how they're looking at it from being in a different place. I was the calmest one in the room and they were clearly harassed by the situation of Jenson not conforming to any of these situations. They were making themselves feel stressed. At the end of it, when everyone cleared out of the room, the lady who compiled all the information was getting very upset, because she wants to help so much, she has a passion to help, and all these kids are struggling. I could feel that she was going to cry, because she wants to do right by everybody.

I said, "This is why you're here. This is your vocation, to make the difference here. This is why we appreciate you with what you do now."

I don't think anyone had said that for a while because she looked just so overwhelmed and upset.

I said, "This is probably not related to Jenson. This is probably because you're facing such a big task and you want to make a change."

She just found that nice. It was like having a hug. She was very pleased that her work had been acknowledged.

I said, "It takes many hours and I fully appreciate it's never straightforward. But it is appreciated, because you are finding ways for us. But we're not always going to agree. And that's not a personal thing with you. This is just me being objective as to what is happening around us and knowing our path forward. It might not necessarily fall in line with your thoughts and that's okay. We need to have differences to appreciate who we are and what we stand for. Otherwise, it would be pretty boring experience."

Focusing on ability not disability

Jenson was doing rehab the whole time during lockdown because he was learning with his sister and his brother. He was not seeing himself as different. He was seeing himself as part of the family, and we were all doing this together. It shifted him a bit more in terms of being at school and not being an outsider, but just joining in with a class. I think that's what he got the most out of it. When he went back to school, he was able to work in a group and take turns.

Academically, he will always show as below target with the usual tick boxes, so I had learnt not to read these reports anymore but to observe and look at what Jenson was actually doing. He seemed to be keen on global issues like Covid and the environment. He was aware of the world around him and how others may perceive his ability to move and talk as unusual.

The word disability feels negative, but we have to constantly fill in forms using this word which can make you suffer with low confidence and self-esteem, and that is just the parents. Jenson thankfully has not had the pleasure of reading all this paperwork. For me, I find it deeply upsetting, when you have to write down all the things your child cannot do. The forms are so clinical, they have no regard for how this could make someone feel when filling this out. Life is already challenging enough, yet you have to jump through hoops to justify how someone cannot do something, so that they can be entitled to some financial assistance.

Jenson was recovering and that should have been recognised within all education health care plans and disability allowance forms. The school had been learning the process but not always communicating outcomes with his therapy team. Being organised with all his appointments and contacts, I would step in and relay information to make sure everyone was updated with the latest medical news. Unfortunately, the Local Authorities are not the same. As parents, we can become trapped in a situation whereby we are not professional enough to give advice, yet we are called upon for information to create reports by the specialists within Jenson's therapy team. Hence, we gave them the information to create the professional report that the school would refer to.

When bad behaviour is a good sign

When Jenson reaches a point of frustration, he articulates very well. One day, after we'd driven to school, ready for a fired-up Jenson to start his classes, we were met with a rather shocking update from the teacher.

She said he'd been swearing.

I said, "What did he say exactly?"

She said, "He threw his glasses down the toilet and then said, "I don't need these bloody glasses."

I said, "Oh, Jenson, that's a good sentence." I was interested with the fact that he'd said that, and he'd said it well.

Turning to the teacher, I said, "Did you understand what he said?"

She said, "Yeah, it was very clear."

When I relayed this incident to the consultant, she was impressed. She was like, "Wow, at least, he's verbalising sentences."

I said, "Yeah, I know, but this isn't good. He shouldn't be saying this word at school."

The consultant just said to make sure he uses nicer words.

Then, I went read a research paper and it said that people who have a pain or something they're trying to get through, to numb it, they often swear. Swearing seems to have an effect on the brain, where it helps ease the burden of the pain. I went, hmm. This might explain why his language is colourful at times, because he's trying to deal with a level of pain that we don't know about.

I thought, where have I done this before? When I gave birth to the children? Oh, yeah.

I'm always amazed at the way that Jenson handles himself. It's good to be able to put yourself back in the situation and have that feeling so you can get a perspective on where he's coming from. There are days when it's just too difficult and I need to have that rest. So I don't ever question it when Jenson needs to rest because I know he's very similar to me. He will keep working beyond his capacity and go into state of exhaustion. I've done it myself, but I can actually stop it.

I'd say, "Do you want to go to bed now?"

He'd say, "No, I hate you."

"Oh, well, that's very good, let's go to bed. Then you can sleep and think about all these things that you're going to hate me for."

"Oh, I hate you. I hate you." And suddenly he's asleep.

This is a reflection of the use of negative language to convey a feeling of tiredness without even realising that this is the underlying cause occurring within the body.

Being a mum, you have to learn to absorb the way in which your children speak to you with such compassion that you are able to see past the actual words and acknowledge what is really going on with them. My children say they hate me at various parts of the day. It usually means they do not want to do something. So putting the investigating hat on, Mum delves deeper into the meaning of this and starts putting together a case for why they may hate me, or the place, action or person. There is an aura of relentlessness, but you will succeed if you use all your senses. Visual clues. Do they look tired? Do they seem distracted? Hearing the words they use, are they positive or negative? Do they need a hug to comfort them through a challenging time? When my kids shout, I talk quietly. When they strike out in rage, I offer them a hug and then I find that either we have a flood of tears or just a calming of the internal anger they feel.

With Jenson, this was an important communication tool, considering he couldn't talk for a long period of time. We still use this technique now and it's just enough to understand what our kids are feeling.

Chapter 7: Food is Medicine

It's remarkable how people don't have any awareness of nutrition and how things that they do routinely every day could have a direct effect on their output of energy.

I was conscious that Jenson needed good nutrition to maintain high levels of energy. This was the only way he would heal his muscles to keep going.

I feel that, in hospital, the importance of nutrition is missed. It wasn't paid much attention to. It was all based on figures. We love to be computer junkies, and feed digits in and get a number that says this is your optimal nutritional balance, but it isn't. It doesn't always work that way. What they worked out and what they gave Jenson meant that there was nothing coming out of him. He was just tired. He was left there looking like a vegetable, and he just needed extra nutrition.

But instead of using common sense, they would go back to their figures, and work out another calculation. Maybe it's because I see the world differently, but I said, "You need to see visual cues. He's asking for more food, but you're not giving it to him. He's hungry." It was frustrating seeing that, but then not being able to do anything about it, because he had to be fed a certain way. I had to have a conversation with all of the team, including the neuro team, to figure out could he eat or not? Could he eat normally?

Eventually, they said, "Well, yes, there's nothing stopping him."

I said, "So why are we doing all of this?"

Food is medicine and it helps Jenson do what he needs to do next. The quality of his nutrition got missed everywhere we went. From the hospital, it got missed. So I had to bring food in and make it look attractive to Jenson. "Look at this jelly, Jenson.

Look, we've got a strawberry smoothie." I was trying to get him to get back his appetite and desire to eat properly again, because he was still recovering and he had to learn how to digest and swallow properly.

It was not so much the fact that he couldn't do it properly, it was more that his muscles needed to get strong enough to tolerate the process of eating. From there, when we transferred to the Children's Trust, recovery nutrition got missed again, but not only that, it was Jenson and 10 other children who were affected. I was getting upset because I love food.

I was saying, "What's wrong with the kids having a good pick of the menu? They've had a traumatic brain injury and brain surgery. Something really debilitating for their brain has happened to them and they need a good, wholesome diet. But what I'm seeing is anything but."

It was appalling. They quite openly said, "This is what they have at the cafe, at the restaurant at the top of the building that all the parents and visitors have. And when they're finished, that's what the kids have."

I said, "But is it what they need to get functioning and regain their proper cognitive function? Are you looking at it going, 'Well, this could be better. We need to put more of this in, more iron, more essential oils to make the brain mechanism work more smoothly?'"

They said, "No."

I was shocked when they broke it down. It was to do with budget, to do with what they had in the kitty to spend. It was sad, because it's so important, but they didn't have anything in the budget for getting good food into the children for three meals a day. It's not asking for much because they're only there for four months. They need to follow a timetable and a schedule of classes, which is their physical therapy and that's excellent. But at the same time, they need to endure the whole day and that's massively taxing. I would probably burn about 500 calories doing a piece of written work. Jenson probably burnt about 2,000 to 3,000 calories just trying to stay still, to focus, to get the pen to the paper, then to try and write, and co-ordinate it all.

There's so much energy being burnt off. It's impossible to even comprehend how much he needs to eat. I just keep the fridge at home filled with good food now.

Listening to the body

Jenson has become so good at going for what he needs. It's almost like he's taught himself, to go for foods that are like medicine.

So if he craves something and it's beetroot or it's an apple or pineapple sometimes, he'll say "Oh, right, I'll have some of that." And we work backwards to figure out what it is that he's missing. Then we piece together a better diet plan to incorporate increased levels of it because he may be deficient. When I go to see the doctors at the local hospital, they go, "Well, how did you know he didn't have enough of iron?" – or whatever.

It was simple. He was going for certain foods and it was telling me that he was short of a certain vitamin or mineral. They were just a bit shocked that I do that much research. But when it's your child, you would. I'd just think, "He's craving these foods," and I'd piece together the puzzle. "Ooh, what do all these foods have in common? Oh, iron. So he's lacking in iron. Okay."

So if I think Jenson is feeling low on iron, I put some more iron-rich foods in his diet, green vegetables, which was kind of rare in our house to begin with. We didn't have any green vegetables. Adam just didn't know what to do with them in a meal. So we had to incorporate them and then it became a staple. Jenson, miraculously, can turn himself around, so that he's feeling better again.

It's not that we are giving him every supplement under the sun or we are asking for a constant evaluation at the hospital. This is him being responsible for himself. Even at such a young age, it's incredible. This is something within him that he just calls on like it's innate wisdom.

I don't know where it comes from, but he's doing his own therapy and he knows what he needs. And it's not for me to tell him. He's coming to me saying what he needs. So I go get it for him. I'm the gatherer. I go get the equipment or the supports or the food, and he does the rest. So I think between us, that's the action plan. And there's no secret, it's just listening to him really and trusting him. That's what I've found.

Chapter 8: Assembling a Therapy Team

This section looks at resources available to you within your local community and social networks, and how to integrate these into home life and school, as well as expanding the therapy programme set by the specialists to be more engaging for you and your child.

Therapy is a team effort and requires your full attention, as the long-term goals will be even further away. There will be a time when you feel useless and not in a position to improve anything for your child, like I felt with Jenson. It took a change of mental attitude for me to address all the things that could be possible for Jenson. Just because he could not do it now, did not mean that he would never do it. It takes time, and the rate of progress for each child in recovery is unique. The position of the tumour, the additional medical treatment they will receive, the side effects of their medication, the tiredness are all factors. There may be long-lasting damage that may not heal and may require further treatment.

What you have that no one else has is the power of love and encouragement, positive reinforcement and lots of energy. When your child sees you are excited about something, they will join in. It is a daunting task, facing the unknowns without an on-hand medical team, but it is not impossible.

Appreciate your strengths

As parents, we are led to believe that we are superheroes who know all the answers to everything. Deep down, we are scared and frightened that our children will never be able to do everything they could do before. These fears are real and need to be acknowledged. It does not matter how many groups you join or friends and family who you invite to have an opinion on what will happen. Even the doctors and specialists will be brutally honest with you that they just do not know. You need to be prepared to face fear head on and keep going. Where there is a will, there will be a way through most situations you encounter.

As my dear neurosurgeon said, "Love will find a way." This was when my son's brain fluid was escaping from the back of his incision site. I tried not to panic, but it was a dangerous situation. When the surgeon mentioned this with a complete calmness, I could not help but take notice and give myself a polite slap in the face. He was right and I needed the reassurance that things would turn out all right in the end. In this situation, it got worse before it got better. My confidence was at an all-time low, but my vision to seek out solutions to everyday problems became a real strength.

Being an innovator through my design work at university, it was clear that I could still create or visualise new ways to do things. When quiet times could be experienced within the hospital, Tadworth communal quarters or Ronald McDonald House, I would quietly draw or write down on paper what I could see as problems and this began to show me a way forward. It's fascinating how we learn the most from retaining information and then applying it later.

Other strengths that I possessed were time management, great concentration and the patience of a saint. Determination and perseverance are necessary, and if you do not develop that at the start of this journey, it will surely be instilled by the number of obstacles that lay before you each day.

When one specialist has one opinion and another has a different opinion, who do you believe? It is a tough one, but negotiating the best outcome for Jenson was all that mattered. So, you learn to take the opinions on board, but not to take it personally. Just because it is someone else's thoughts, be they professional or personal, does not mean you need to let it affect you and where you would like to see you child's recovery going.

Every now and then, there will be a person who will make you feel so frustrated, angry, annoyed, sad, bereft and not knowing what to think that you could quite easily retreat into your shell. This is okay. Welcome the opinions, because one day, you will find the way to go forward or the person you need to contact for the next stage of recovery. If you want to cry, then allow yourself the time. It is not a weakness. You are just letting out some intense emotions that have not been heard but are stored within your body like a lead weight. Afterwards, when you have used the last tissue in that box and your head hurts, drink some water and realise that it was just what you needed. The next day will seem lighter, and you will move around quicker, and your appetite may come back. So, eat that breakfast, start the day as you mean to go on, with high energy.

Understand your vulnerabilities

Jenson's weaknesses were his levels of tiredness and concentration, and his balance and co-ordination, with one side of his body experiencing delayed feedback. The sophisticated movement of walking would take a lot of preparation by working on all the milestones a little baby would face in its first year of life.

I would always experience intense emotions if anyone spoke negatively about Jenson. It would cut like a knife and reduce me to tears. I had learnt not to react with such volatility in front of the kids, but when I was alone it would be another story. There are diverse ways to cope in traumatic situations and some of these include drinking alcohol, smoking, eating sugary foods, indulging in a complete pity party for one and shutting out your partner.

Take your pick of prescriptive drugs for sleeping and depression, and you have the perfect storm of losing yourself. The best gift I could have given Jenson was to be present every day. Whenever the urge presented itself, I had a choice, do I eat this cake or should I just take a walk? If I fancied a drink, I would ask myself, am I going to be at my best in the morning? If I answered no, then it was enough for me to change my decision to a better one. Of course, if we had a break at home or had family looking after the children, then an odd glass of wine would be okay, just not the whole bottle or two bottles, which could lead to discipline going out the window and me slurring my words and getting into petty arguments with my partner and close family. If you combine this with sleep deprivation, it is not the best solution to de-stress, quite the opposite.

Ask for help

So, what other weaknesses lay lurking in the wings? Asking for help and talking to others were the next ones. It is a lonely place to be in when your old life no longer fits in with your new one. Those drinking friends disappear when you thought they would stick around, your family suddenly is busy every time you need a chat. In the end, you get so sick of being by yourself, that you start to find others to connect with. The awful feeling of being alone with no one to talk to got unbearable for me. I was not going insane, and I wasn't depressed (well, at least I didn't think so?). I had just isolated myself without even realising it.

So, as I mentioned, I faced my fear head on and looked at Facebook and started to accept the numerous group invites that I had ignored over the months. It was apparent that there were others going through a similar experience and I began to feel a sense of purpose. With each day, I would check in online and see what the other families were doing and how it was working for them. It gave me a direction to take and someone to reach out to.

Amazing charities

The **Danny Green Fund** is an amazing charity that no one had told me about, but I came across it through researching posterior fossa syndrome. They were so understanding and acknowledged all the frustrations we faced. I wanted to empower Jenson, so I set about attending the various disability exhibitions mentioned by the charity and our physiotherapist.

I did not want to accept that Jenson was disabled and wanted to find ways to help him move about.

Kidz South is a major exhibition held annually that demonstrates the latest in disability innovation, technology, help and guidance. It provides a tsunami of information dedicated to helping you find solutions for your child's particular mobility situation.

This exhibition had everything you could think of and helped me to understand ways in which Jenson could be struggling. It was not always easy to see that, but it was enormously powerful. We found out so much information, but more importantly, we realised that Jenson's particular syndrome was rare and needed specialist interventions. His recovery mimicked difficulties like cerebral palsy, yet it was not permanent and was likely to change. This fluidity was a curve ball with equipment. As soon as I could get funding for it, Jenson had already moved on to the next stage of recovery. We had to be one step ahead of him and think of the next pieces he would need. By thinking ahead, you were able to attain equipment that would last longer and be more beneficial.

A **Tomcat Trike** caught the corner of my eye and Jenson was in pure shock, with his eyes doubling in size, when he saw it. He was excited, and the passion I had to get him moving made this Trike a must-have. But how would we be able to afford it? It cost an eye-watering amount because it was so niche, but we both wanted it, so I took the details and went home to think about it.

The Danny Green Fund, the charity that helped us through endless chats and compassion for our situation, stepped in and funded the Trike. I cried with such appreciation that someone out there wanted to help us and we were not alone. I thank them every day for the joy this Trike gives Jenson. If I could take more photos and videos I would, but the thing is my hands are always busy holding on to one child or two, and shaky hands mean a blurred image. So, at this point, I would hope that this lovely charity will understand why I cannot update them all the time.

I think the therapy team was surprised at how much I was getting Jenson into, because I suppose maybe their perception of parents was that they're not that bothered. They're waiting for everyone else to do it for them. I wasn't one of those, I was diligently creating a plan to get as many different sports, different movements in as possible that we could actually do.

They were surprised by it, because they said, "What does he do at the moment?"

And I said, "He does this, this, this, this."

They said, "You do all of that."

I said, "Well, this is why he's like this now, because if he hadn't had those things, then he would probably still be struggling to sit up properly."

The horse riding he does is very disciplined. It's everything he hates, because you must do as you're told, but he does it and benefits from it. With swimming, if you don't do things right, you're going to sink. So you really need to know how to float, which he loves doing. A good friend of mine has his own martial arts studio, and when he wasn't using it during the day, he allowed me and the kids time to do some simple exercises with him. Sometimes, it's helpful to just get Jenson moving around. It was brilliant, because he could just roll on the floor and it was very safe.

You and your child are a team

Working together as a team is really important, I can't emphasise that enough. Just because there's an age gap between you and your child, it should not define how you work together. It's about working with your skills and their skills, or how they are in the moment, and pulling them together and then evaluating how you can be better. So it's an exchange of skills. As I was a therapist, this was good news for him, because if I'd been in another profession and didn't have any knowledge like that, it would've been a lot worse. Because of the contacts I knew and the facilities, it was a game changer for him. He needed those things and I needed this fearless approach.

Working together as a family

This year, we will be coming up to four years since Jenson's diagnosis, and when I look back over what we've done and all the things we've experienced, the most important thing has been family, and our values as a family. You've got to have the same values within the family, like trust, honesty. And you just have to believe in the same goals. We might have different ways of achieving those goals, but we have the same belief system. And as long as we all believe that we'll get there, we will eventually get there, even if we don't know how long it will take.

Throughout our whole experience, I have noticed that we share the same values as a family. Determined, stubborn, relentless in achieving our goals. Leading with honesty, intuition and integrity. We listen to one another and take ownership when things go wrong. Never shying away from responsibility, we work through our problems as a team. My children love playing together, but they also respect each other's private time to be by themselves. I call this thinking time a period to self-reflect. Whenever an argument may take place, taking time out to understand why that happened works well for all of us. This is like an emotional marathon that you have to complete on a daily basis.

Part III: Coping Emotionally

Chapter 9: The Five Stages of Grief

As parents, we are never really taught how to prepare for life's curve balls, especially when it involves our children. We roll from one day to the next and are expected to just suck it up. Be strong, you have this, superhero, you are so amazing. Okay, have I said enough cliches? For once, I am going to say, it is okay to not be okay! Forget those beliefs that your family, friends, doctors, other patients and healthcare professionals are saying to you. There will be a time when you'll just want to cry, you'll want to scream about the pain of injustice and howl for the life you used to have. This is all completely normal and a process we come to realise as grief.

Denial

This is the initial numbness and lack of any emotion felt at the time of diagnosis. There will be upset and you may cry, but you have not begun to deal with the effects this will have on your mind, body and soul. You are fuelled with adrenaline and fear, which propels you into action and results in restless nights of broken sleep and a mind racing with questions. What I learnt from this denial stage is that it acts as a form of protection to keep you from facing the actual loss experienced. In my experience, it allowed my family to get through complex decisions and work out a way to cope and maintain a routine for the other children. I think you may have heard the expression "It's business as usual"? Well yes, it is as you do not have a clue what is about to happen. Sticking to what you normally do regulates your stress levels. In some ways, it buys you time to figure out your next steps.

At this time, you may feel estranged from your partner, because you both handle shock differently. This is okay, and if I could go back and tell myself this, it would have made all the difference – especially when people are telling you how to think, feel, react and behave. We do not understand that they are only trying to help. Your own parents are normally a good guide to turn to, but in this instance, they are in as much shock as you are. It is a lonely time where you are walking through a fog, but this does not last forever, as you will move on to another stage.

I like to think that this system is circular and that all elements are interchangeable, so one moment, you can be in denial and the next you can explode in anger at the mention of something connected to your child. Nothing is linear about how these emotions are experienced, so don't put pressure on yourself to act a certain way because a book, leaflet, website or specialist told you that is how you will feel.

At this stage, you are still talking to others and filling them in on the situation. This will seem like a full-time job.

"Let me know how he's doing."

"Why didn't you tell me about this?"

"Why are you shutting me out, you never tell me anything?"

Do these demands seem familiar? It is because of the shock that you will instinctively want to tell all the close family and friends involved. The problem is, once you start to do this, you will have even more work to do to keep them updated with the slightest change in the situation.

A few things that helped us in this predicament and that we recommend are:

1) Put your phone down for periods of the day (for example, breakfast, lunch and dinner), and give your children and partner your full attention. Be present and give yourself space to just be.

2) Set up a group page for those friends and family who you want to keep updated and update them this way. It will

save time as one post will update everyone, instead of you sending hundreds of messages out or making those phone calls that were only supposed to be five minutes but which then turn into an hour. You will be exhausted by all that is happening around you, so why spend that last moment frantically calling that distant relative when you could be getting some rest?

3) Withdrawing from everyone is okay, this is rest time, so use it to recharge. The medical team will encourage you to take regular breaks. Leaving your child's bedside is okay, as the nurses or healthcare professionals will often be only too happy to help and step in while you go and freshen up. Take turns with your partner to go out and grab that meal or a change of clothes.

Bargaining

This becomes a period of restlessness.

"If only."

"What if?"

"What could've been done differently?"

If you cannot accept what happened, it will only turn into anger and guilt later. Walking through every decision you made and then rerunning different outcomes is the mind's way, but it is self-destructive and torture of your soul. I kept a journal and when I look back at this time in our lives, it affects me deeply that I was so terribly hard on myself. In life, we experience some terrible events, but we grow from it and learn to appreciate how resilient we can be.

Signing the paperwork for Jenson's surgery became a source of guilt for me, and looking over the papers repeatedly did not help me to acknowledge how my son was so ill. It made me despair that I had even allowed a surgeon near him. But then common sense prevailed. It was as if someone had slapped me in the face to make me wake up to the reality of the situation. This was the wake-up call. What were your other choices? Then I had the lightbulb moment, there was not another option, the only other option was death! So, I chose life for my son, and what was wrong with that? The fact was that I could not accept that sometimes our choices come with consequences. In our case, this is a life-long spectrum of disabilities for Jenson, with no certainty of him ever regaining the skills he used to have. Surgery is not a holy grail and it is not always perfect, but it did save our son's life, and for that I am eternally grateful.

Sometimes when we listen to others, our view on what happened can be distorted. Google becomes a wonderful oracle of information, but it can make us begin to question and doubt the decisions we've made. What if our son's tumour was caught earlier on? Would he have had a better chance of full recovery? These are tough questions that I used to ask myself every day. No one could give me the right answer because there isn't one. How I got through this period was by understanding the science and the actual presentation of Jenson's tumour. He had a small percentage of tumour that remained within the brain stem, and all the books I've read on the biology and neuroscience of the brain indicated that operating close to the brain stem and causing the tiniest damage would have resulted in what is so eloquently described as 'incompatibility with life', also known as death. The truth was there. It would not have mattered if we'd discovered this tumour earlier, as it was still growing out of the brain stem and would have required the same kind of surgery.

I convinced myself I had done the right thing because I needed to, as I was a mother desperately trying to help her son, while taking care of her newborn baby. I even went as far as to go back to my pregnancy with Jenson and evaluate everything I did. Did I work too much? Was I eating the right foods? Was I too stressed? Truth be known, all those things could have been better, but that was the best I could do at the time. It did not help that the doctors and surgeons repeatedly kept asking me questions about the birthing experience of each of my children. It was like they were trying to connect dots to a potential genetic cause, but this all came to nothing.

All that information had to be constantly relived as I was asked to fill out yet another form. Boy, I was ready to explode with anger and that was perfectly normal. An extreme invasion of privacy was happening, and not once did they ask if I was okay. I WAS NOT OKAY!!! In my mind, it was like they were trying to pin the blame on something or someone. My bargaining period was well and truly over. Both boys were still alive, and my daughter continued to go to school, so we had everything to be grateful for.

Depression

It was clear that what we could tell ourselves daily influenced our outcome. By becoming more positive and optimistic, our energy levels increased, and I could keep up with all the round-the-clock duties of housekeeping (yes, we still did this while staying in hospital), eating, drinking, researching, contacting friends who could help, attending the pre-school and baby groups, making sure that my daughter had enough help at school, parent evenings, school nativity plays and justifying why my child was absent from school (seriously, filling out these absence forms was a pain in the ass).

It was not long before I realised that I was at rock bottom, feeling worthless, low and a complete failure. I'd look at everyone else, and they seemed so damn happy and enjoying life. I did the worst thing you could have done. I began to compare myself to others and that hurt. It hurt that my baby boy spent his first year of life in a hospital. All those Facebook stories of your friends looking so happy and celebrating their new baby's first birthday. For me, I was just glad I could spend his first birthday at home with his brother and sister. We tried to have a lovely party, but deep down I was at rock bottom. I truly hated myself for what had happened to us. I could not bear to look in the mirror. Where had I gone? I was feeling isolated and withdrawn, but most of all I just felt sick for no reason. Something needed to change.

This time is about exhaustion, as both your mind and body are spent. There is nothing else you can give. The effort to just get out of bed becomes a challenge. However, I had three little reasons to get up each day and they relied on me, so with every fibre of my being, I fought this low mood and started to tell myself I was good enough and that this time would pass.

I would look at myself in the mirror and say what I would like. It was like introducing myself to my body. Hello, this is me, this is my incredible body which gave birth to three children. Here are my wounds. I have earnt every single one and I love them. I love how my shape is curvier and my boobs are bigger. This is a mother's body. I embraced the even more sleep-deprived dark circles under my eyes and my chaotic bed hair. It was all part of being a parent. Wash and go, minimal time to get ready in the morning. I was like a beautiful warrior setting off to do battle with the day's challenges.

With each positive comment, I could feel a spark of self-confidence. The woman I used to be was getting fired up. Let's go and tackle some villains today or, in my case, just face the villain's downstairs at breakfast!

After acknowledging to myself that I felt low and uninterested in the outside world, it was as if I was being shown the way. A friend on the school run popped up on Facebook with a suggestion that I join a running group. This was a scary thought, "I mean look at the size of me." To say I had put on a few pounds was kind. I was obese, and everything was hurting, my back, my knees. I felt heavy. But putting my fear aside, I prised myself away from home and drove to the group. Gosh, getting up early to run was not a love of mine, but with a goal set, I made it happen.

It was the best decision I could have made. Not only were the ladies welcoming, but they were also easy to talk to and motivating. The first few sessions were difficult as no part of me had moved this way in a while. But being a swot, I looked at other ways to enhance my training and worked with a programme at home. And yes, the kids joined in too! Mum is exercising, so I will do the same.

Jenson saw this as a positive change and it made him want to move more. This was amazing and made me feel positive for the future. I was influencing him, so what else could I do?

Well, you know how this story goes. I ran, and I ran. I ran for miles upon miles until I realised that my son wanted to earn his own medals instead of wearing mine.

I used running as a way to show Jenson that if you try hard enough, you can move your body a little better each day. Every time I ran at an event, like a 10k road race, 15k Dorney Lake challenge or the Bracknell half marathon, it was to set the intention to my family that if you want something, go and get it! I loved running to clear my mind, but I loved it more as I could give Jenson my fantastic finishers medal afterwards. He would be screaming my name as I ran around the corner and I would be frantically searching for him as I crossed the line. Every race showed him what he could do if he puts his mind to it. My body was physically showing him what he could do.

Initially, I did not have any real goal to achieve, but then I started to set some and here I am with one marathon behind me. Not only did running help me to lose weight, it saved me from those awful low moods. I looked and felt good. The depression was lifting and a new me was emerging. The funniest thing is that you don't need to run for very long to feel this buzz of endorphins (the feel-good factor). It was the combination of the great outdoors, good company and enjoying a hobby that I used to enjoy as a child that helped. It was a second chance to get some enjoyment and love back into my life again.

Finding a sport or doing something you love allows self-expression, and for me, that was what I needed. To express what I had been feeling and let it go. By the time each run ended, I felt lighter and problems were easier to work through as I had more energy to deal with them. On an even more positive note, my children were also getting involved and having fun.

Anger

The outbursts of uncontrollable rage, when your patience snaps and that fearsome loud voice reverberates in a room. I knew my anger and it was not going to be contained. There are moments when you feel ignored, you are not listened to and are left out of meetings. When the experts start telling you all the things that are wrong with your child, call it a mother's protective instinct, you begin to show up. Right, you have had your turn, now I am going to take mine.

Every time I would head into a meeting with a panel of ten professionals, it was challenging. They would present an imposing if not intimidating stance, go off and talk about how experienced they were, and you were left thinking, do my opinions count for anything? Anger can be motivating at times and my anger forced me into action that affected change within my family's life.

Stepping back and taking the time to listen to the experts, and then sharing your views, however hard that is, is 100 percent better than getting angry. To curb the emotional outbursts, I would listen to music before a meeting or an appointment, or I'd set an intention to be accepting of any information that was presented. Writing down my questions, and any current observations or problems experienced, also prepared me for talking about my son.

I used anger as a positive, to feel empowered. It is not a shameful thing if you can harness that energy and put it into doing something constructive, like filling out that long application form for Disability Living Allowance (DLA for short). Focusing that energy into completing the most mundane tasks allowed me more time to spend with my son and his physical therapy sessions.

With each passing month, there will be times when you will rage about how your life has changed so much, how you have so much to learn, how nothing ever seems to be finished. Does this sound familiar? It's like the first time you have a baby. Each frustration is completely normal, but give yourself a break. No one will know how to live this new life but you, so take the time and go through each obstacle as a family, because together you can get through anything.

Whilst in this anger, you can find yourself exhausted. You cannot stay this way as it is unhealthy. Rest and drink plenty of water. Walk off the excess adrenaline before you head home or to the place you may be staying. We often say things we do not mean whilst angry. Never be too proud to apologise, even if the people around you understand that it's your anger speaking, not you. It is for your own peace of mind to realise that you were overwhelmed with emotion.

Recognising anger is the first step to accepting and working out ways to control your own personal levels. It will improve communication with the medical healthcare team around you. The local authorities and education system will be triggering. So, look after yourself by being as calm and informed as possible. If you are unsure, ask questions. This will leave you feeling reassured and not anxious about the next steps within recovery and daily life.

Acceptance

Wow, this particular aspect is still ongoing for me. While acknowledging that your life has changed forever, it remains difficult to be at peace all the time. Where you have hope for a full recovery, the reality is always somewhat different. What my experience has shown me is to accept things as they are, at that moment in time. My son will not just suddenly walk by himself one day, it will take an enormous effort and numerous therapy interventions over many years to achieve. But it is not impossible. We have to be patient. Patience is a quality that does not come easy.

Tolerance also becomes a strength. When you go out into the public, you will face many occasions when you feel like it is too hard. The physical challenges, the equipment, the unexpected behaviour, people stopping to chat, people staring at you and your family. You need to understand that it is curiosity and by acknowledging them, you will feel easier about it.

Journaling

I kept a good journal during that time. I had to write in it daily, because there was so much going on and so much stuff that wasn't the best that I'd ever seen in the hospital either. It was so upsetting and journaling became the go-to for me.

At Ronald McDonald House, there was a communal kitchen and a living area, but we all had our own little en suite bathroom.

It's kind of like a scaled-down Premier Inn. It's really nice that they could offer it, but there weren't that many rooms. I remember being there every evening when I would come in around 11.30pm, because that's when Jenson used to go to sleep. I'd have to just write, write, write, write for about 15 or 20 minutes, because it was just that upsetting. Then I could sleep. If I didn't do it, I couldn't sleep. I would just lay there wide awake, waiting for 6 o'clock, so I could get up again. It was a mad and condensed eight weeks. Trying to unpick it all and go through what actually happened in those eight weeks is revealing. Because a lot happened, when I read his medical notes. There was lots going on all the time, there were a lot of tests and a lot of unanswered questions.

Normally, I can deal with things quite effectively, but journaling allowed me to just brain dump everything, but sort of in a positive way. I wanted to put everything down in a written form because I was in two minds about whether I would seek legal advice because of the treatment and how it all came about.

When you're emotional, you can't really think straight. So I made all these notes anyway, but I didn't have a clear idea of where I was going. In the end, they just became notes that got put in a folder and got filed, as I didn't want to do anything negative. I think the overall picture was to do something good and it didn't sit well with me to do anything like making a legal case against the hospital.

It was not the best time and also it didn't feel right either because I'd need them for so much longer and Jenson's condition is life-long. When people do seek legal redress, it tears them apart, because you have to really go into minute detail about every single thing that happened. And you're dragging all your surgeons, your doctors, your consultants into it. They're going to remember that. They're human. They're not going to not remember that. So I didn't want to do that. I wanted to build a team, not cause destruction. I think that was the thought behind it when I changed my tact. So I wasn't an all-out-attack mum in a very big protective mode going in every morning, picking them apart. I just became more of a team member and just started chipping in.

So for me, that was massive, because I saw things differently. I saw how they worked differently. I don't know why it shifted like that. It was just that I could see that they were struggling within the NHS. They're always struggling, but at this point, I could see how much. There were all these emergency cases coming in and they all had neurological problems, and then keeping up with the daily chores of looking at records and making sure everyone got all their medications, and staff not turning up. It all became very apparent that it's not efficient.

If you just sit there, things are going to get worse. So you have to take action. So that's when I decided, yep, I'm going to chip in and do whatever you haven't done. I'm just going to get it done.

So if you haven't washed him, I'm going to get whatever I need to try to wash him and do everything like that. It definitely made life easier because I was contributing and not just observing. So I felt less anger about the situation.

Chapter 10: Support Groups

Support from other parents

For parents whose child is in hospital for a long time, it's a very tough experience, but they are brilliant, very strong people. They have to be, even though they may not think they are. Some days in hospital were just absolutely shit. The parents would all rally around and help each other. There was a sense of community. Let's call it hospital life on the ward. Some ladies would pick you up and go get you a drink, and others would be, "Oh, we've got these sweets." It was just everyone looking after each other. We would help by watching someone else's child if they had to step out. So the community was like a safety net, because you have more eyes on deck. It's not just you.

So you're able to relax a little bit and that was gold. I just didn't realise it back then. You've got that other person who doesn't know you, and who you don't know that well, but you're bound by the same sense of seriousness with your children, so you are happy to help each other. I just can't describe it. It was such a compassionate thing to do for each other. We thought nothing of it. It was all mums together. The dads would turn up during the day, but they were on their laptops doing the work. It was mainly mums and they would have their moments at night, just sitting there contemplating what's next? You'd sit back and watch it, and think, "Wow, we're all in the same boat. We're all having these feelings, so it's not unusual and it's okay to be like that."

Then, you find that you are a bit further along in the process. Say you've been doing hospital life for six weeks and then someone drops in for their first week, and you're like, you need to go and do this. Have you had a break? Suddenly, you are the one who's taking over the nurse's role.

You'd say, "You know what, go and have five minutes, go chill out and have a coffee, take a break.

They'd say, "No, I need to be here."

I realise that I was like that. The nurses must see this all the time. There's nothing like hitting that note and realising, "Oh, I was so bad. I was so rude to them, I was this, I was that". So I was massively grateful to all the nursing team there.

The kindness of friends and strangers

I remember when this man who I knew at the football club where I volunteer part-time, one day, gave me a discount using his discount card. I wasn't expecting it. I said, "Oh, thank you." It just made me feel a bit gooey, all this kindness. But when that was happening with Jenson, I felt like we were getting a team together. They were like Jenson's little management team, they all wanted to help him move forward. There were all different sorts of people. We had acupuncturists. We had my friend, Jon, whom I share the clinic room with. He was helping and would come and do a little bit of acupuncture with Jenson and play games with him, like Lego. He said, "I wish I could do more."

Then one day, Jon said, "I think this might be a good idea. Let's do some fundraising and get Jenson this set of headphones that are really good for his motor co-ordinating movements. We could give it a go, because it's kind of like me doing my work with acupuncture, but I don't need to be there. He could wear them and it will still do something similar."

I said, "Okay, all right."

Then within moments of him posting online how he'd been helping Jenson, because he has a very astute brain for marketing and happened to be well connected, he just knew when to gauge the audience on Facebook, people just started donating to get these headphones.

I said, "You are wonderful. How did you do that? It's like you've got a magic wand."

He said, "We just want to help. That's all."

All these wonderful people are right behind us. They want us to get Jenson as well as we can get him. They see that we are determined to push as far as we can with finding the right equipment and access to therapy, to get him where he feels he's at his best.

That meant something to the family because it came from Jon, and I didn't ask. It also came from my client base. One of my clients set up a GoFundMe page and donated some money. I didn't ask.

She said, "This is to start it off. With all the help you've given us over the years, this is the least we can do. We just want you to be back into the groove of yourself and your family. We know how much it means to you. We know how hard everything has been and we just want to be there. So, if we can't be there, we need to offer our help differently. And maybe this fundraising page for your son is a way for us to say thank you for helping us, but also to give you time to work with your son. Because, financially, you just never know how that will impact you and your career."

My client base had been watching these events unfold over the years and they're still there now. There's a good 100 of them who either just ask if we need help or support Jenson by commenting on his Facebook page. "Oh wow, look what's happening with Jenson." They're still interested. And sometimes I can't believe that. The community are all waiting for when he takes his first independent steps. To be honest, so am I.

I set up a Facebook page called Jenson's Journey, while he was in hospital to update my friends, family and clients on how he was doing. I had a Go Fund Me Page just after he left Tadworth Court. We raised nearly £3,000 to help with his rehabilitation costs. With the funds, we invested in riding lessons, swimming lessons, one-to-one tutoring, orthotic suits, hydrotherapy, muscular therapy training, equipment for eating, walking and balancing. We provide updates when a milestone has been reached or there has been a breakthrough with a certain area of difficulty such as speech and word formation. Currently, it's updated once a week.

I always think that they're not going to want to know what I've been doing. But I put it on Jenson's Facebook page sometimes that I've done this run or that run. When the London marathon came about, I was raising money for different charities, including Sebastian's Action Trust. They came up trumps again, didn't they? Friends and clients started donating, but I was out running, I couldn't see what was happening. I thought, "We're not going to make our target. I've tried my best, but it's a bit difficult. Everyone's suffering with the pandemic situation and they haven't got much to donate."

But I was wrong, because as soon as I was out there running, sweating to death, that's when all the donations started coming in. My phone was going ping, ping, ping, ping, ping, ping. These were emails from people donating, and when I got back and I was in that pain zone of like, "Oh, what have I just done to myself," I looked at how much I'd raised.

It actually made me cry a lot. I just thought about all the kids who were in my head to make me do those last six miles. I knew how much it would mean to them. It even included Jenson because he's in that charity too. They do a lot for him. It just made me feel really humbled that they're always sort of there supporting us.

We have a network of people who we surround ourselves with who champion our successes and support our failures as we learn from them to fight another day. A network can consist of a group you feel a part of. Most families who have a child with a brain tumour set up support groups and this helps parents to ask real questions and to let off steam when social issues or the educational system has them backed into a corner. I am a member of some of these groups led by The Brain Tumour Charity, The Danny Green Fund, Ronald McDonald House and Sebastian's Action Trust. With these groups, my family can just be themselves.

Part IV: A Father's Perspective

Adam's Story

When Kim phoned me at work, I felt worried and shattered. It was like one minute my head was in work, the next minute Kim's taking Jenson to the hospital. I was thinking, "What the hell's going on?" Worried sick, I was trying to wrap up work, so I could get back and be there and help. Obviously, I wanted to be there for Kim and for my son. So I rushed over to the hospital. I found Kim looking very worried. The nurses were all making a fuss of Jenson, because at that point in time, he was still a nice bubbly little boy. The diagnosis of his brain tumour had not really registered.

When they told me, it was like there was suddenly no air. I couldn't breathe. I didn't understand fully. I don't think I understood fully until I saw him after the day the main surgery, when he was completely motionless. That's when I think I really understood what we were going to go through. But before then, it was just like, "Okay we're going to have this bump in the road, we're going do some surgery and he's going to be all right." I always try to look for the positives. So I was trying to think positively.

I couldn't cry. There was no tears. There was no emotion. I felt like saying to myself, "What's wrong with you? You've just been told your son could die. He's got a tumour." But I think it was such a shock that I was wondering to myself, "What?" Then they told us that we had to go to the hospital up in London, to St. George's, for an emergency scan, and that Kim and Jenson would have to go off in the ambulance and I'd have to follow in the car with Mason and Sophia.

At this time, Mason was still a newborn baby basically. So I was juggling that and then obviously the stress of everything and having to find a hospital I'd never been to before, and then trying to reconnect with Kim and Jenson once I got there. That was a bit stressful on its own. When we got there, there were more doctors, more nurses, lots of questions, lots of people saying this, saying that.

Then we had a lot of waiting around until Jenson went for his scan. But one thing that stuck with me and will always stick with me and always makes me a bit tearful is when the doctor said that if we had waited any longer, he probably would have been dead. So that was a pretty hard-hitting moment. But I've raced forward a little bit. There was a moment back in Frimley Park hospital, where I was changing Mason in the changing room, because he had done what babies do. I just had a little moment when I looked down at him thinking, "Wow, you're so perfect in every way and then thinking Jenson is just in the other room. He is perfect, but now there's this huge problem." So I did have a bit of a cry then I think, and I gave Mason a hug. I get emotional thinking about it. Jenson went off for his scan. There were loads of doctors buzzing around and you just felt like a spare part. Just doctors here, doctors there. There was so much stuff to take in. I still was thinking that we weren't going to be there for long, or at least not for nearly as many years as we have been, let's put it that way. I was thinking maybe a year and we'll be out of it or something like that. Jenson had his scan, and they confirmed that the tumor was there. They were going to put a button in the top of his head to release the pressure, and then they would do some surgery where they go down through the brain and open up the ventricles or something – I can't quite remember the terminology they used – so that the brain fluid could flow down the spinal column. The surgery happened that night and I was blown away by how quickly it was all happening – scan, brain surgery, bang, bang, bang. It was so quick. We obviously stayed the night at the hospital. I think it was the next day that they let us go home, because we argued that we needed to get some home time before Jenson went in for the big operation.

He was also quite bright at this point, because obviously, it was like someone had taken the weight off his head. He started dancing around, having a whale of a time again and being like his old self. I was at home with Jenson. Mason was there in his cot. I think Kim had gone out with Sophia, because I was at home on my own with the boys. Jenson had his bandage on his head and he was looking at me with his dummy in his mouth, and he was walking up and down. I was really feeling how great it was, because he was walking up and down. He was talking.

I said to him, "Walk up and down", and he started running up and down. I said, "No, don't run just walk," because I was worried that he was going to fall over, especially with this new button in his head, but he didn't. Then I said to him, stand on one foot and he came up to me and stood on my foot, and it made me laugh. I said, "No, not stand on my foot, stand on one foot." So then he looked at me, put his arms out and his leg out, and he stood on one foot and balanced on one foot. I was thinking, "That's amazing". I videoed it, so we have a record of it. It was just really nice and I felt so positive about it, thinking, "We've got this, it's going to be great."

He started slowing down a bit. But then I just thought he was maybe getting tired and needed to rest. They still had him scheduled for the big operation the following Tuesday. So the weekend was about preparing childcare arrangements and talking to my parents about looking after Sophia, as I didn't have a clue how long we would need to be in hospital. Mason would be with us as he was just a baby. We went back up to St George's and we talked to the doctors, had meetings. They talked about this and that, said this, said the other. It was basically, if you don't get the surgery done, he could die because this hole keeps healing over. The tumour has to come out, it's the only way forward. They were telling us it was not cancerous. So that was quite a big relief. We were thinking well, okay, as long as it's not cancerous, we can sort this out. We can get on top of it and we will be all right. And he'll be fine.

So fast forward a little bit. We went to this waiting room, which was opposite the intensive care room, where they said Jenson would be once his surgery was finished. I went with him and they gave him gas and air, and put him under. That was quite emotional, thinking he was going to go off to have surgery. We went to the waiting room. It had horrible green seats and they were uncomfortable. It was quite a big room, but it was just nasty, a real, proper, clinical place.

I just remember the room having this horrible negative feeling about it, like everybody in there was sort of looking down and looking worried. It was not a nice place to be. That was our home for a couple of days, I suppose. They had these bunk beds out the back, and showers and things like that. But they were all run down. They weren't well kept. We were so tired we went and had a lie down every now and then on the beds, but they weren't very clean. So yeah, it wasn't great. We had Mason in there with us and I was thinking, this is no place for a baby.

I think even Kim said to me, "This is no place for a newborn baby." We were both thinking it and saying it. It was just horrible, but we were there.

He's out of surgery

Some time went by and then the doctors came in finally and said, "He's out of surgery." It was like five hours later. But we had to give it a little while for him to come round and for them to do their initial assessments and what not.

Then we were allowed in to see Jenson, which was an emotional moment. I felt very excited, but we weren't all allowed to go in at the same time because we had Sophia and Mason with us. So we had to take it in turns, like shifts. I'd go in for a little bit, then Kim would go in, and so on. During one of these turns, I went in and they were talking about his pain levels being a bit high. He kept writhing around on the bed and asking for a toy bus that we had brought. He was playing with this, but kept writhing around a lot, arching his back and doing funny things. He wasn't co-ordinated. He was sort of all over the place. It wasn't our normal Jenson, but it was still Jenson, if you know what I mean. So I thought to myself, well, he's moving and talking. This is great. This is good, it's positive.

Because they thought his pain levels were really high, they started pumping morphine into him and he started to calm down. He looked like he was having a little sleep. I thought, he's probably really tired after all that's happened. His heart rate was still within normal parameters. When you're in a situation like that, you're red hot on all that's happening. You're watching each beep. So then it was Kim's turn. Everything looked fine when I was there. So I walked out, and me and Kim talked for a little bit, and I settled Mason with a bottle. Then Kim went back in to see Jenson and an hour or two later, she came back out crying and really upset and looking hurt, with a distressed look on her face.

I thought the worst straightaway. And it kind of was the worst in a way. She sort of muttered it. She didn't fully say it. She said,

"No, his heart slowed so much because of the morphine, it pretty much stopped."

I said, "He is all right now?"

She said, "Yeah, he's all right now because they've stop giving him the morphine."

So that was quite a heavy time. There were lots of up and downs, like the worst rollercoaster you've ever been on sort of thing. And obviously we still had to deal with Mason, and everything else.

Jenson settled down and stabilised, and then the doctors did loads of tests. They were testing all the time. I think he was on PICU (Paediatric Intensive Care Unit) ward for about a night and a day. Kim had to stay there. I had to go and sleep on my sister's sofa, because they wouldn't let me stay at the hospital. Only one parent was allowed to stay. So then I had to go and leave Kim and Jenson. That was really quite hard. I felt like I was betraying them, because in my mind, we do it all together, through thick and thin.

There are levels of intensive care. PICU was the highest level of intensive care that he was on at first. Then they moved him to the step down unit. He was up in that ward for a little while and they were pretty good up there. They looked after him quite well. He was just sleeping all the time. He wasn't doing a whole lot. Then we had the posterior fossa syndrome talk and they said that he had a complication on the surgery side of things, and he'd got this posterior fossa syndrome. I'm like, I don't have a clue what that means.

Kim was talking to them. Kim's so good with all the jargon, the doctors. She could be a doctor herself if she wanted to. If she had the time, but then she just rams her life full of everything else. But if she had the time, she could be. But she knew what they were all talking about. She knew the ins and outs of it. I think she even did a little research, but at that point in time, she knew everything and I was just lost. Then they said, oh yeah, he can't move. He has to relearn how to move. So, basically, it was like looking at a doll on the bed. Jenson was just lying there. All he could do was move his eyes. He kept looking at me and Kim intensely with his eyes because that's all he could move. It was heartbreaking. It was really hard. That was the moment when I realised we were in for the long haul. This was not going to go away. This was not going to be fixed in a year. This was going to be years. That's when it first really hit me.

I asked them, "Can I pick him up?"

They said, "No, you can't pick him up."

I said, "But he's my boy, why can't I pick him up? I picked him up when he was a newborn, why can't I pick him up now?"

They said that he hadn't got any muscle tone. There were too many wires. I could hurt him, I could do stuff in his neck. Obviously, where he had the surgery was right in the back of his neck. So they were worried that if I picked him up, I would cause problems, issues, ruptures, something. I don't know. So they said no, basically. So I was like, okay.

Flicker of a finger

It sounds weird when I say it. It feels like a week, but it might have been longer, went by being in the hospital, sitting next to his bed, getting Kim tea and coffee, and just trying to live in a hospital, which is horrible, because you've got no creature comforts at all. It's just hard. You can't just go and get something to eat quickly. It's not nice. It went on for ages. Then one night when I was sat there with him watching him, it must have been ten at night, maybe later, and I just saw his finger move. I was so excited. He moved! It was like a revelation. I called Kim in, and then we both got our phones out.

We were videoing Jenson move his finger. We were really quite happy thinking, oh wow, it's all going to come back. It's all going to come back now. Then the next day came around and he was laying there completely still. We thought, oh, nothing's happening. Then the next night, he moved his finger again. But he moved it more. Every night, he was moving a little bit more. Then it happened in the day for a week and then maybe his arm would twitch.

When his eyes were open, his finger or his arm would move a little bit. We were all like, oh my God, he's moving, it's daytime and he's awake, and he's moving again. Then the movements at night would get bigger. He'd move his arm or he'd thrash. Then the next day he'd be moving more. It went on like that for months, until he was able to sit up a little bit with the help of a cushion and he could move his head. That slow progress went on for a long time, for months.

He had other complications where he had to have all this pipe work in his head, because he'd got an infection in his brain fluid. Then they put this contraption on him which we had to monitor and it had to be level with his head. The nurses kept putting it at the wrong height and it would drain his brain fluid too quickly. Then we were like, no, and we'd tell the nurses off. "You put it at the wrong height." We were vigilant. You had to be because the nurses were doing their best, obviously, but they had all these other people to see to. So we found ourselves becoming an advocate. We learnt what that machine did and we learnt how to use the feed.

We learnt what every last beep meant. In the end, we were almost more qualified than some of the nurses. We were telling them what they needed to do. So then the shift would change and you'd get a new nurse and go, oh, this is this, and this has to be level, and he has his feed at this time and he has that much. So it went on like that for a good while. I remember that Christmas came, and one day Mason was sat on the bed with Jenson, punching him in the head. Kim has a video and pictures of him annoying Jenson and Jenson punching him back, or at least trying to anyway.

One big thing happened during the first Christmas after his surgery. We wanted to take him over to Ronald McDonald House, it had became our residence to help us get across to the hospital each day. People would laugh at me because I would be wearing shorts and a t-shirt when there was snow on the ground. But when you got up to the top floor of the hospital, the heaters were stuck on full blast. So it was like the tropics up there, and everyone was sitting there sweating. Everyone was looking at me as if I was nuts, because I was wearing shorts and a t-shirt, but it was better than sitting up there all day sweating away. My parents and Kim's family took turns to visit and the Ronald McDonald House provided this neutral space for us to just be together.

We had all sorts of ups and downs. I was always having to go back home, leaving Kim and Jenson at the hospital. I didn't like doing that, but it had to be done because Mason was too young to be there all the time and Sophia had school. There was loads of toing and froing, and lots of driving. And lonely nights. There were a lot of lonely nights, where I was either stuck away at home or stuck in a hospital somewhere on my own.

At the time, Kim and I didn't have much of a relationship, we were just working. There was the odd moment that we had to ourselves, but it was mostly just like work, because we had to do so much. We were like ships passing in the night. At Christmas, we managed to convince the doctors to let us take Jenson over to Ronald McDonald House. We had to go for a test to make sure we could change his feeding tube. Kim and I both passed, there were no problems. We'd seen it done so many times, it was ingrained. So then we could take him over to Ronald McDonald's House, and that was the nicest evening we'd had together as a family for a long time.

Super Mum

A lot of it was just, what's Jenson done, what do we need to do for Jenson, how's Jenson? It was all very much focused on him. I was focused on him, but I was also thinking of Kim, because Kim, like I said, was putting her heart and soul and every last ounce of energy into Jenson's recovery. She's so amazing with it all. I was so happy that she is his Mum and I still am to this day. I said to her only the other night, "I'm so happy that your Jenson's Mum, because you're so good at all of that." When we go to a doctor for an interview, she knows exactly what's going on, what each doctor is doing, who each doctor is. She just reels it all off and I'm there going, how on earth do you do it?

That's like ten pages of information. Kim's just got it stored on the tip of her tongue and in her head. I'd have to go and look it up or write it all down. She just reels it all off. I suppose she's done it so many times, it's just like second nature, but she is an amazing person when it comes to that.

Some people think that I'm her rock, but I don't see it like that. I see it that she's my rock. I'm just trying to keep the sand around the rock so that it doesn't get knocked over. That's how I feel about it. I suppose sometimes I feel like a bit of a headless chicken running around trying to put everything in its place.

I did a lot of that back when we were in the hospital, because it'd be like, you stay with Jenson and I'll go off and sort out Mason, and I'll do this and I'll do that. I'll grab some food and I'll grab us a drink and I'll do this. I can't sit still, I'm one of these people who has to do stuff all the time, which really annoys Kim. I'd be making things or doing something, and she'll be like, what are you doing now, aren't you still going to do this and that. Then hours would pass and she'd say, where have you been?

Well, for a lump sum of the time, I was lucky enough to get paid and not have to be at work. But when we went over to the rehabilitation centre at Tadworth, I had to have a meeting one day with the boss, because he wanted me back working.

I said, "Well there's no chance. I can't. Well, what do you expect?"

My old boss was one of these men who'd just go, well he's been in hospital, he is fixed now, he is out now and it's all done and dusted, I need you back. He didn't get it at all. He still doesn't get, even now, I don't think. A little while ago, I said, "I've got to go to the Royal Marsden hospital."

He said, "What, you're still going to the hospital? I thought all that was done now."

I said, "What are you talking about? It's for life. He's got to go to the Royal Marsden for six monthly check-ups."

So I had to sit there with him and discuss everything, and he made me feel awkward and under pressure because he was like, "You've got to come back because I need you to do this, that and the other."

I said, "Well, I can't, can I? How can I? My son comes first."

I always used to say to him that my family comes first. The fact that I had to keep telling him that just said to me that this man doesn't get it.

So when we were at Tadworth, I had to go back to work three days a week, which kind of worked in a way, but also put a lot more strain on Kim, which I didn't like. But I couldn't not do it because I was worried that I wouldn't have a job to go back to. I wasn't the main earner, because Kim can earn a lot more than me in a short period of time. But my job was just the bread and butter money, it kept things ticking over. It was a steady income and all that. So I was worried about what we were going to do for money and how we were going to keep a roof over our heads. There was loads of pressure – on me and on Kim.

Going back to work three days a week was weird, because one minute I was in full rehab mode with Jenson at the rehab centre, and then the next minute, I was at work fitting someone's windows in their house and it just felt so removed. It felt sort of disjointed. It was a bit of a head screw, like an outsider looking in trying to get my head round it. That was difficult. There was also a lot of driving back and forth to Tadworth. Then we had problems with the care at Tadworth, where we didn't feel that Jenson was being looked after properly. There was nothing prepared for the parents at all at Tadworth. All there was just a room to sleep in, a living room. You didn't get any food as this was for the children only. So we had to shop at the local supermarket. Ronald McDonald House brought in food for you to sustain your energy during the day and they really looked after you there, so you could concentrate on looking after your child or whoever was ill.

At Tadworth, it felt like they didn't want the parents to stay in the room with their child. You were often told to go off and do what you need to do. We were like, well you're going to look after our boy. They were like, we'll look after him. We were separated in different living quarters.

So one day, Kim went off to, I think it was to Asda or somewhere to get some food for her and Mason, because she had Mason with her all the time. When she came back, Jenson was screaming his head off in the bed.

She said, "What's going on? Why is he screaming in his bed?"

They said, "Oh, he wouldn't calm down, he wanted you, he wouldn't have any of it."

Kim said, "Well, that doesn't sound like Jenson, but you still should have tried to calm him and see to him, and you shouldn't just leave him screaming in the bed on his own."

That night, I said to Kim, "Well, just bring him home, just drive him home."

Driving back and forth to Tadworth

I've done more driving than Kim, so I didn't think anything of it, really. But it was a big challenge for Kim, driving. We had quite a new car at the time, but it was a small car. She had to try and get all Jenson's stuff in it. The car was rammed to the gun holes, with Mason, Sophia and Jenson, prams and assistance equipment. But she managed to get it all in and drive there.

She said to me only the other day that she was worried about driving all that way and I was like, you never said at the time. Tadworth was not around the corner. You need to take one of the motorways and she was proper bricking it. She stood up to that challenge, took it head on and did it a couple of times, and was nervous, a bit scared. This was mainly to do with Jenson and Mason being passengers. Jenson was still very fragile and could not protect himself if you had to brake suddenly. The seat belts offered some support but not enough for his poor muscle tone. So you had to drive carefully at a consistent speed. Then she said that after doing it a couple times, she thought she could do this every day, just drive there. It would be fine. I was used to driving, so I was a bit thick there and didn't really realise what a strain it was for her. I was thinking, "What's wrong with you?" I was taking sort of a bloke approach, I suppose. So that was interesting to find out only the other day that she was that worried about it. So you spend all that time with each other and you still find out things that you didn't know.

So she was driving up and down to Tadworth. She did the second half of the week and I did the first couple of days. I was working three days a week, but all the time, my boss was going on at me, "When are you coming back four days a week?"

I replied, "My son is in constant rehabilitation care at Tadworth."

To drive Jenson home we had to take a test to use one of the assistance vehicles. So I went on a driving test and passed it but thought it was more of a legal requirement rather than a test of my skills on the road.

We had to put this collar around Jenson's neck. We've still got it now, it's in his bedroom somewhere. It was a funny little collar thing that you strapped around his neck to keep it still whilst you were driving.

That was nerve wracking, because you had to remember that Jenson had no muscle tone, so if you pulled away too fast, his head would go flying back. Or if you'd brake too fast, his head would go flying forwards because he couldn't stop himself. So it was an added pressure when we were driving Jenson around. He was like a precious cargo. But we did it and it was fine. We came home for the first time after all those months and months and months in hospital. Jenson was so happy, he was rolling around on the floor with his brother. My friend Mikey came over. Mikey had known Jenson since he was little, so he knew him before the tumour. I didn't see it, because I was too busy looking after Mason and running around doing stuff, but Kim saw the look on his face. She said he looked the most shocked she'd ever seen anybody.

Kim said to me, "You should have looked like that when we got told in the hospital." But I was beyond shocked when we got told in the hospital. I was thinking that it wasn't happening to me. I felt completely sort of removed.

I suppose we would have been shocked too if we'd seen a little one-and-a-half-year-old bouncing around, riding bikes, jumping, playing ball, and then saw that he could now only just about roll over on the floor.

So then it was just physio, more physio. One day we were at a session and he rolled over, and I saw that he'd pulled out his feeding tube. Normally, we would need to do little tests every now and then to make sure the tube was in the right place so that there was enough stomach acid for digestion.

The tube had come out so many inches. It was basically barely in, it was at the back of his neck somewhere. The rehabilitation centre was not a hospital, so there wasn't always a medical team on hand to respond immediately. So we took out the tube, and Kim and I just looked at each other and said, "He's going to have to eat solid food now, we're not putting that back in."

So we just said to Jenson, "Right, this is a good chance to make you eat solid food." I think he was quite happy about that at the time, because before we got to Tadworth, they did assessments of him on the ward. I remember one day, we got pictures of him sat there holding this chocolate muffin with a big grin on his face, one-sided obviously, and all covered in chocolate.

He just got on with trying to eat solid food, bless him. He didn't refuse. He didn't struggle. He just saw the food and started eating. They were all amazed.

They said, "How did you get him to do that so quickly."

We just shrugged, "He's Jenson, isn't he. He's like me and Mum, we just get on with things."

Thankfully he has the same mentality. He just gets on with it and gets it done. So we're very happy about his mentality and his outlook on life, his attitude to life has helped him out massively. We reckon that if he was like Mason, he'd scream and make a huge fuss about every little thing.

Jenson's attitude helped us through

I don't think we would've got through it. So he helped us, which is quite interesting to think about in the whole scheme of it all. To think that he was helping us with his outlook, which helped him to a point. If you fast forward to today, he's getting up to mischief, fighting with his brother, causing us trouble. He gets around the house like no tomorrow. He did a 5k walk the other week, the Santa Dash.

So never give up. Never. You will feel like giving up and you will feel distraught, but have the belief that your child is going to be all right. I always had the belief that Jenson was going to be all right. I think that helped me get through a lot of the stuff. I couldn't think about what might happen. I always thought that he was going to be fine. Give it a week, give it a month, give it a year, it'll be fine. That's how I've always looked at it. I never looked at it like he's not going to make it. So that helped me, I think. I never dwelt on it. I just always thought that he was going to be all right. We're going to make him all right, Kim and I. I thought about the possibility of death three times maybe in the whole time. Once when the doctor told me that if we hadn't brought him in, he was going to be dead. That was when I thought about death and that was hard. Then I thought, well, now he's going to be all right, we've caught it in time. We're going to be all right. So I went back into that mode of thought and then when they told us about the posterior fossa syndrome, I thought about it a lot then, because he couldn't move anything.

He looked just like a rag doll. I was thinking, "Jesus, it's like he's dead." He wasn't dead. But it was like he was dead, because there was no life in him. He didn't say anything, he didn't make any noises, he didn't move. I was thinking, "My God, you're trapped. This is horrible." I only ever thought about death a couple of times.

I suppose I have a positive mental attitude. I know that's an easy thing to say, but I just never thought it was not going to work. Does that make sense?

We're not phenomenal. We're just average Joes. Well, maybe not average Joes, but we're just a standard mum and dad who want the best for our kids. I'll do anything and Kim will do anything. So they come first. I wouldn't say we were anything out of the ordinary, not super parents or anything. We just love our kids and want to do the best for them. Others have said that to me before, "How did you cope with it?" I don't know, we just got on with it. What else can you do?

If you don't get on with, what happens? Well, things fall down around you. Mason's nappy needs to be changed or Sophia needs a new uniform for school or Jenson's feed needs sorting, right. If you do nothing, it's still going to be there to be done. Problems are still there. You still have to do all these things. So we just got on with it.

Two single parents

We were two single parents. That's about the best way I could describe it, we were both single parents going through this. We were together. When we were at Ronald McDonald House, we had a room where we could spend time together. But we were rarely in that room because we were always with Jenson. So it was like being two single parents, especially with night shifts. Leaving Jenson was hard, because you'd have to leave him up on the ward and go down to Ronald McDonald House. You'd feel guilty and you'd feel bad, and you'd be worrying if he was all right. You'd be listening out for the phone, because they'd ring through if something was wrong. That was the same at St. George's through to Tadworth. At Tadworth, they put us in this little house that was nowhere near where Jenson was. It was almost a ten-minute walk to get to him.

Tadworth was horrible. The therapies in Tadworth were great, but the rest of it was horrible. The hospital sold it to us as, "It's the best place ever, it is so great there. They look after everybody, you can relax. They've got nurses to look after him when he's in the room." It was absolute bullshit.

I hate that place. Whenever I go past it, I have a deep hate of that place. The people who did the therapies with Jenson were amazing. They were great. The teacher even came a month or so later to his new school just to see him and to see how he was. That's how good the therapists are there. But the level of care outside of the therapy was not acceptable. I think Kim and I were viewed as the voice of the parents at that place.

Kim complained, "There's no fucking fruit on the table. There's no food for the kids. What the fuck." She basically told them off. Told them they were not doing their job and that shit.

The next day, there was fruit on the table. Literally, the next day, and I remember another parent saying to Kim, "How did you do that?"

She said, "You just stamp your foot and shout, you make yourself heard."

We've always done that. We're not scared to voice our opinion or put our two pennies' worth in and ram it home. We don't care. I suppose we've been through so much, we just don't care anymore.

The other night Kim said to me, you haven't written anything for your chapter of the book. So I just sat there and just wrote and wrote and cried, and wrote and cried, and wrote and cried. I was like, wow, I feel so much better after doing that, because a lot of those memories, I just put in a box. I put it over there and I got on with what was in front of me. Yeah.

Like last night, I bathed Jenson and then got in bed with him, and just lay there with him. It was quite nice because I hadn't done that since back in the hospital, I think. I just lay there with him and I fell asleep with him in my arms, and then woke up later on and he slept well that night. I did that quite a few times in hospital, stayed in the bed with him. In Tadworth, they didn't let me stay in the bed. They got a mattress and I lay on the floor next to him. I didn't want to leave him on his own. He was just a little kid and especially with all the problems he'd had, I didn't want him waking up in a strange room with no one familiar around. I tried to see it through his eyes and how I would feel if I was him. I knew he'd be worrying himself.

Part V:
More Curve Balls

Chapter 11: Miscommunication

Jenson had this bad cough and sore throat. We'd just moved to this big new house, and it was exhausting. We called in some help from our friends and family to get the move complete. We had so much to do and not enough eyes to watch the boys. So, getting injured was a high risk and coupled with the stress of not knowing where anything was, we achieved that we thought we wouldn't get completed. And then Jenson was back in the hospital with a high temperature and vomiting. We didn't know what was wrong with him, so they tried to figure it out with tests. The hospital was saying to us that his tumour had grown. I was actually sitting there listening and thinking, hang on, you might have got this wrong.

I didn't feel like that was what had happened. Somewhere information must have been misplaced. I don't know what made me think this. I just thought, you've got it wrong. I didn't feel like there was something bad going to happen. It just felt like they'd got it wrong. So I had a chat with the doctors at the hospital and because there were two or three hospitals involved with Jenson's care, they hadn't got all the information from the hospital we were dealing with at that point in time. This is why it's so important that you keep notes. They assumed there was something growing in his brain, which really wasn't the case because the other hospital was saying that was not a growth, but actually scar tissue. Because the Royal Marsden consultants weren't present at the meeting, they pressed the panic button.

The hospital insisted that we had to get Jenson sorted out. I was the one saying to them, slow down a minute, you've not got all the information and you are going for something that might not be what you think it is. So I disagreed with their assumption, okay, we need to wait for the call from the other hospital, but they didn't want to wait. They were being impatient, they wanted to obviously administer medication for Jenson and give him steroids. There wasn't any information, not to my knowledge, but they had seen something from this scan and they wanted to act. Then they booked him for an urgent MRI. So we were in London again, that one day, just before Christmas. This is when I got the phone call – note that it was me getting the phone call, not the hospital.

The Royal Marsden was calling me, "Oh hi. We're just calling with regards to Jenson. We wanted to catch up and see how things were going?"

They were asking me, "Is he on the steroids? Did they administer them yet?"

I said, "Yes."

Then they said, "Oh, he doesn't need to be on them. What we are seeing is just the same as it was before from his scan. It's stable."

I said, "Okay."

They asked, "Where are you?"

I said, "I'm at St George's, we're just having an MRI scan."

They repeated, "You're having an MRI scan?"

"Yes."

That was The Royal Marsden hospital. Then they went off to go and tell the local hospital their good news. Guess what? I'm sat there in a chair, at St. Georges, because Jenson's in the scanner, thinking what are they going to say when he comes out?

They bring him back. "Yes, we did the scan, there's nothing there. It's good, he's good, you can go. You don't have to wait around, we're happy."

Jenson was just coming round from the anaesthetic, grumpy and sitting up trying to eat and drink, feeling a bit out of it. He was just so moody, because it was coming up to Christmas and he wanted to be at home. And he was all good, and we were thinking, "Wow, amazing, this intuition skill works."

If your gut feeling or detective skills suspect something is off, then you should always ask some questions and re trace your own notes. How was the last scan? When was the last scan? What have the school been dealing with regards to sickness? Could it be something else causing these symptoms? Well, that was just it, it was a case of the seasonal Norovirus with a well-timed throat infection like tonsilitis. The outcome was eventually fine. I was trusting myself more, Jenson was stable, we could go home. We're going to have Christmas together as a family, well almost, I needed to check on my Mum. It was a while since she had got in touch, and I was starting to get concerned.

Without kicking up a fuss, not only was I a full-time carer for Jenson, I was also a carer to my Mother. In fact, I was a carer to everyone apart from my two brothers. As the years went past, Jenson was getting older, and I never appreciated that my mother was finding life very hard. The week previous, I had been to visit her, and she had had an accident that involved a few items of furniture falling on top of her. Without wanting to point the finger, I had a strong suspicion that the cat had got under her feet resulting in a rather painful fall.

Between me and my mother we tried our best to get her up and sat down, but this was so difficult. I had to fight my way through the door to get through with all the furniture blocking it. Then I had to make the call, the hospital needed to look at my mother's wounds and assess her for more help at home. Being a proud woman, she refused and that left me and my brothers with some problems of how to best look after her. We worked out a plan of taking a week each, but it became too much. I could not handle the extra hours on top of all my other responsibilities and Mum was just getting worse.

I had felt nothing like it, total insomnia and zero energy. Jenson still required me to be on standby during the day even though he was at school and Mason was at pre-school for a couple of hours. My daughter was in the last year of primary school so my whole day revolved around driving here, there and everywhere. Between us, we had to arrange several health appointments for my Mum. The time and waiting list were ridiculous but we kept the appointments. It was so sad to have the news that she was almost blind because of the size of the cataracts in her eyes. That day was awful. As I took her to the appointment, we had to use a wheelchair to get her around. Her legs were so weak. The prognosis wasn't great, her only option was surgery and that was something she did not want to do.

All the communication between me and my brothers, the hospitals and the care team kept me up until late at night. I had become so involved that I forgot to tell the school this massive pressure I was under. Cracks were beginning to show, I could not keep going like this. The school was complaining that I was late collecting the kids, I was late getting to work and hospital meetings for Jenson, and the pre-school thought I had forgotten about Mason. What a total shit show. Something had to give and in some ways my Mum being in hospital took a lot of worry off my mind. She was in safe hands or at least I thought so.

Chapter 12: Not the Christmas We Were Expecting

I finally got Jenson home, everyone was home. Brilliant. Except that my Mum was in the local hospital for treatment for a foot infection.

We have Christmas together as a family, but my Mum doesn't phone us. She always phones us at Christmas, she has never not phoned. I took it that there was something seriously wrong. I had a totally different sensation in my gut, in the pit of my stomach, this time. I was feeling awful. I really didn't want to do it. But I knew on Boxing Day, because I couldn't get hold of her, that I had to go to the hospital. Everything was delayed, but we had to build ourselves up for something, because we knew something was going to happen. I went to the hospital and initially they said that I wasn't allowed in because of the Covid cases. I thought that because she was a bit older, a senior, she'd be in the elderly ward, but she wasn't, they'd moved her.

So from talking and negotiating with the staff at reception, I said, "I need to go find out if she's all right, because she's not taking any calls and my family, my brothers and sisters, are worried sick." So they agreed and let me in. They told me the ward and I went up there. It was on the off chance that a surgeon came out and said, "You do know this is a coronavirus ward?"

I said, "No, I don't." But when he told me that, I felt like I'd fallen down a hole, "Coronavirus?"

"Yeah, it's a Covid positive ward."

He was abrupt. Because obviously he was military and he wanted to get the job done.

I said, "Well, can I have someone come out and speak to me about it, please?"

He said, "Have you got a relative here?"

I went, "Yes, my mother."

He went to get somebody, but they didn't come out quickly, it took what seemed like a lifetime for someone to come out and speak to me. When they did, they told me off for being there.

I said, "But I'm here because the reception staff told me to come up to this ward so I could speak to my mother. I didn't know it was a Covid positive ward. Now, somebody please tell me what is going on here. My Mum was in here for a skin infection on her leg. At no point did I get told she had Covid. I certainly didn't know she was positive."

They were mortified.

"Nobody," I said, "Not one of you in this hospital called me or a next to kin, or my brother to tell us that our mother has Covid!"

She pulled me into a side room and started talking.

My attitude was, "I'm not going anywhere until you tell me what is going on." I've never felt so serious in all my life. But all she was telling me was to leave because it was highly infectious.

I said, "I've only got one mother. Now, if this was you, and you only have one mum and someone was telling you this and you wanted to find out how she was, you'd be sitting here, fighting her corner."

She said, "I know I would."

I said, "So don't tell me I can't be here. I'm entitled to be here." I sat there and I wasn't going to be moved. I was Jenson in this moment. I was just going to sit there until I heard what I needed to hear. And it wasn't good news. She'd got it and she'd gone into this sort of non-responsive state.

They'd failed to tell me any of this. They were very, very apologetic that no one had been called.

I said, "When you tell me this, because I'm close to my mother, I know we haven't got long. You are telling me she's going to be okay. That's rubbish. I know that. And all I am disgusted with is the fact that you think she's on her own and she isn't. I need to tell her children."

It started to come out of me like I was a third person. "I have to go and tell her children. She has six children, she has 10 grandchildren, she has a big family. I have to go and tell them that she has got Coronavirus and it's bad, because let's face it, she's unresponsive. I don't think she's going to come round. And you are telling me this to soften the blow, but I know deep down she hasn't got long."

She was trying hard not to cry herself.

I said, "I've got to be ruthless with this, to get this into my head, to then go and deliver this. I only came here because I had an impulse to come here because no one was answering my calls. It has been the biggest shock of my life."

Apart from Jenson and all of that, this was a shock because it was unexpected. She went into hospital for a minor thing. It was a skin infection she was being treated for. We all assumed she'd be back out again. She was going to spend Christmas with us and that wasn't the case. Instead, I had to go back home, knowing full well that within a small window of time, she was not going to be with us anymore. I had to somehow tell everybody that. In that moment, it was just like I felt when I'd been given Jenson's diagnosis. It was just a shock and I was just feeling hollow. Because you know all of this information and no one else does, and you've got to try and convey it in a way that they can understand what happened without them thinking you're strange and have mystical powers.

I actually went there through intuition and instinct, because I felt that something was wrong. When I told my brothers, they broke down. Everybody was just lost. Usually, we didn't even think Mum was that much of a glue for the family. But in that moment, when I told them, she was the glue all right, she was the roots. They were beside themselves. I wasn't prepared to be hit with the emotion that was coming out. I was sort of looked on as the bad guy. I was just trying to find out what was going on. I knew that even though she was still there and she was still breathing, she needed me there because she was scared. I had to be there, and I wanted to be there because I thought, "You can't be on your own."

This was a pandemic. I understand all the risks now, I'm fully appreciative of that. But I was negotiating with the hospital to have a bedside chair next to her. I said, "I'm going to gown up with the gloves on, mask on, the lot. But I want to be next to my Mum. I don't want her to die alone, I really don't."

The hospital staff were initially resistant to it, but then they made an arrangement where she could be in the side room so I could be there. And my brothers could be there to say their goodbyes. If I hadn't gone in there to negotiate, she would have died alone. Then no one would have known until later when they had to inform somebody. That was the biggest shock I'll never get over, that they just had no inclination to tell anybody. It played on my mind for ages.

Why didn't they think to call? I was so grateful that I went there, even though I felt uncomfortable, like something really bad was happening. It meant that I could help, I could say goodbye to her. She wasn't alone, and the passing she had also helped me and my brother to have a bit of closure, because it was such a quick turnaround. It was Boxing Day, and then on the 29th, she was gone. There was little to no time. Jenson was out of hospital, and I was celebrating Christmas and being happy about that. Then I was there in this well of, "Oh my God, I'm going to lose my mum. I'm just waiting for the phone call." It was such a shift, I was up and down at the same time, but I got prepared. The only reason why I could do that was because of my family and the way my kids are, the way Adam is.

Adam just stepped in like a rock. He just said, "What do you need? "

I said, "I don't know what I need, I have no idea."

He was just there, on high alert like he does, being super dad when things are going a bit wrong.

He was like, "But what do you need? I can help. What do you need?"

I said, "Adam, I just need you to be at home with the kids. I've just got to go."

He knew when I went that my Mum wasn't coming back and he had a cry. Obviously, from being with him for seven years, he'd grown close to her and he knew what was happening.

He said, "Okay, I'll stay here." And he kind of exposed the emotion for me, just how sad it was, because she spends Christmas with us all the time. Because we are the nearest to her, we'd always get a place ready for her. She'd come and mess about with the cooking, the procedure of cooking the turkey and things that have to be done a certain way. The fact that we were not going to be doing that hit him. So, when I went to the hospital, she passed away just like that as I held her hand. It was soft and starting to feel cold, because you can feel that life force slipping away, it just changes. I just told her it was okay and that I've got it, I'm going to make sure everything will be fine.

Everything that she asked for I did and I stuck to it, regardless of what everyone else thought, and made sure that her wishes were met. I think she realised, because she could still hear, that we were there. Then she just held onto my hand very, very tightly. And then she let go and she was gone. The nurses came in, and they were really shocked, because she was walking around two days before. She was telling them how she was going to come out to our house and have dinner. She was really happy she was coming out, and she was going to see the kids.

They were saying, "Oh no, no, not Christine." And they confirmed, "Yeah, Christine, she's gone." They were just very, very upset and they offered help, asking if we wanted a drink.

I couldn't move. I thought, I can't drive or anything. I just don't know what to do, and nobody teaches you how to deal with a death of a parent like that, especially that quickly. I know that sometimes it's even quicker for others, but what happens in that moment? How you do things was just a massive learning curve. My brother was just crying. I obviously was very upset and was just trying to tell people, and all I could think of was how her hand had just slipped out of mine. Just like that, she just let go. In fact, she was in pain for a long time and it was just freeing, she was just free to go. Whatever I said to her and how I said it must have just been that final thing she needed to be at peace. But it still hurt and was massively sad, because Jenson thought she was coming out of hospital. He knew she was in the hospital because he had been in hospital for part of that time as well. I was trying to tell the kids too. How do you tell them? Because they've always had a strong bond with my Mum.

It was not easy. I just couldn't say anything, I had no words. I got back, I had her bag of things, because you have to take their things with you. I had the presents and things that I got her and some of them weren't opened, and it was just incredibly sad. I left them in the car, because I just couldn't take it. She was always so strong. She was the first to complain about anything. Whenever there was a slight illness, she'd be there beating the doctor's door down and having a right shout-out with anybody, trying to get it sorted out. It was like I'd lost my best friend, who was also a big part of Jenson's journey. She was the silent but strong person who was always there. She just knew what to say, when no one else could get through to you. There's always one person, and she was that person.

It was never sugar-coated with her. She would just deliver what she had to say in the bluntest fashion. She would be just like, "Get yourself together, what's wrong with you? You can't carry on like this. When life kicks the shit out of you, you still got to get up. You still got to look after your kids, you got to be there for them. You can't stay stuck in this mood."

That motivation was exactly what I needed to get me out of those low points, even though I thought it was quite unpleasant at times. But when you say goodbye to your best friend, it is the saddest time.

I thought about all the moments we spent talking about silly stuff and just going out and having tea, nothing fancy. We'd have tea at Tesco, just spending that quality time together, buying absolute nonsense from the shops. It was never anything on our list.

I'd say, "Why are you buying that silly thing for Christmas, that laughing, talking Santa Claus?"

She would just burst out laughing, saying, "Well, it makes me laugh, listen to it."

And she'd be pressing the button, and it would be singing away. Just for that moment, I'd be absolutely mortified that my Mum had such poor taste in shopping. She had that capacity to distract you in that moment. And I thought, oh my God, she did it on purpose.

All the thoughtful things she did just came to the surface. It was that wave upon wave, all this unconditional love she was giving you. It wasn't to give you a hard time, she was actually loving you in a way that she knew you, and you just didn't see it. She knew I cared about her a lot, but the way I heard it was from all the nurses. They were saying how proud she was of me. All this stuff she never bloody told me, she told them all. That she was proud of what I was doing and how well my son was doing, and they knew all about Jenson. I was like, wow, I haven't even met you guys before and yet you're telling me, "She was so proud of you." I just went to pieces, I just couldn't believe it.

Then I got annoyed. Well, how dare you. You never told me that at all. And now you've left me and now you've told everybody, and now I'm hearing it from them. It was the last laugh, I guess. But I went home and I felt very different. I felt loved, because all those years I didn't feel loved by her. I actually felt loved and appreciated and respected, even though it never came from her. But when the nurses all started talking about it, it just blew my mind. She did love me, she wasn't being hard on me. She was just trying to be that strong support, which was unwavering, just so that I could steer myself away from any trouble and get back into the calmer waters. Thanks Mum.

Chapter 13: Mum's Legacy

Once I achieved that, I lost her. It was like the end of a big chapter. It was going to be a massive change. We're going to lose people on this journey, and it's going to hurt. You lose your mother and then obviously we were in that stage of uncertainty. How is this all going to work out? How are we going to manage the funeral and speak to family whom we had not seen in years? But we did, we managed it. And it was a touching tribute to a lovely lady. I think organising it helped, but knowing that my Mum had said how proud she was of what I had achieved with Jenson, when she was in the hospital, that helped me too.

It gave me the strength to carry on doing what I needed to do next. It really shapes your character, because there's nothing worse than losing a parent. Part of you dies with them, for sure. But for me, in that moment, I felt that part of me was being freed to go and to live my life like she wanted me to. It was very different. I felt lighter and almost guilty that I felt in a good space and was able to get things in a way that I was comfortable with, and I was happier with in my life and was not feeling any judgement or anything. It completely turned itself into a positive experience, and I wasn't prepared for that because she was my best friend and I'd lost her.

But going forward, it was a massive, massive thing to teach me that I could do whatever I needed to do. I had everything I needed and it was like she was saying, "You don't need me anymore, you've learnt all your lessons, all I can teach you, and it's my time to go." But it's never easy to let go. Since then, one of our neighbours has also passed on. They were very prominent with Jenson's chemo journey. They were also suffering with cancer, then death came along to claim them and it was equally as devastating because it was another person in our battle who was no longer there.

You have to learn to accept death as much as life, because it's all part of this process. Jenson's illness just made it even more real, with what he was going through and what he must be thinking, especially with the chemotherapy and what the outcome could be. You can try to protect everyone as much as you like, but the reality is that you can't. When you lose one person, and then you lose another, you're like, where is this going to go?

Lifeforce

But something really beautiful happened, and it was that the life force, it seemed, went back into Jenson to get him through the chemo, to stabilise everything, to give us what we have now, which is a stable time of his life, where he can get better still and recover even more.

Mum would always say to Jenson, "Why are you moaning that you can't do it? Of course, you can. You can do it, Jenson. I can see you. You are getting better all the time. You're getting stronger." She was such a supportive reinforcement, but she made herself invisible. It was just such a bizarre dynamic to have. But it was the way she chose to be. And instead of trying to change her, I let her be, because she let me be. That was our relationship. She hated me at times. So what? It was the same with me. Ditto. I'd go out thinking, I can't believe somebody would just buy so many little pointless things as treats. But she was teaching me humility. You never go around to someone's house empty-handed.

You've got to be grateful for all the people in your life and thank them for everything. Whether that's the hairdresser, the person at the surgery who books your appointments, the person who delivers the food to your house, the checkout person at Tesco. Just say, "Thanks."

I now take that on as a very important quality and instil it in my own children. And it's getting through. In their school reports, which explain what they've been up to, the teachers say how polite and well behaved they are. And it makes me feel very emotional, because that came from my mother and I'm passing it on. And when you get that back, you think, "Wow, she's still here. This is awesome."

Letting me make my own mistakes

Unfortunately, my mother didn't have the energy left to see the results of all the good things coming. But I know that I carry her in my heart anyway, because she's there every day. She'd probably be super proud that I officially started my e-commerce website, Muscle Mechanics, selling my blended aromatherapy balms and that I am living my own life, without having other people dictating how that should be, and being as free as I can. This was something she never really had. It's a gift. So by not being controlling of me and letting me make all my mistakes, she actually allowed me to be who I am now.

If she had steered me in a direction, I don't think I would have landed all these lessons so well. They were painful, but essential. It is sad that she's not about. But I respect the fact that everything has a time. And that was her time last year. It was in the sweep of the Covid pandemic. I just knew, when I did that hospital walk, and they said that she'd got Covid, that there wasn't any comeback. She wasn't coming out. That was a big thing. Saying goodbye to someone you loved dearly is one of the hardest things you ever do. And I was privileged to do it. So when I said goodbye to her, I promised her that I would do my best to go after everything I want to do and not give up on it, because she wouldn't. She'd be behind saying, "Go on."

Laughter is the best medicine

The Christmas after I lost Mum, I found myself in B&Q, and it had the most ridiculous looking reindeer that was singing Christmas tunes. I was laughing hysterically at it. Adam thought something had happened to me, I don't know, like I was possessed by something.

He said, "What is wrong with you?" And he kept pressing the buttons on this toy.

I said, "You're not helping, actually. You keep pressing the button."

The ears were flapping on this reindeer, and the bells were ringing. I thought, "I'm going to get one."

Adam said, "Why would you buy something like that?"

I said, "I'll tell you later when we get home."

It was just something that reminded me of my Mum. I thought, "I'm going to buy this, because it is quite funny." Then, I picked it up and put it in the trolley, thinking, "It's starting, isn't it? Oh no." So I started putting stuff in the trolley I didn't need, the Christmas splurge, just like my Mum did.

Taking on positive challenges

I can't describe the pain and the hurdles that we've had this last four years. It's like a soul being branded with an iron, because those emotions are so raw, but you have to carry on, you've got no choice. You have to keep going. Your kids keep you going. Life keeps you going, it kicks you out of bed in the morning because you've still got to keep doing your thing. So many times, I just wanted to curl up in a corner and not bother. But from everything I had been through already, I knew that wasn't the way to go. I needed to do something, so I set myself ridiculous challenges and one of them was to do the London Marathon .

Then I thought, let me book in some more runs and train myself up to this big event. In a way, it's therapy talking about what we're doing with Jenson. Exercise was also doing the same thing and it got me in this good space. If I hadn't had that, I wouldn't have got through the first part of the year. It would just have been a brick wall. I don't think I would've got to this point.

Part VI: Jenson

Chapter 14: Jenson's Relationships with Himself, Family and Friends

What do you see when you look at me?

Waking up, I feel a sense of uncertainty. Going back to school after a lovely holiday.

The pressure of having to figure out how X+Y= Z, without really knowing why?

Why should I be made to feel different?

Why do I have to conform to a certain X, so I can be ticked as Z?

Every day, the same Y haunts me. People stand and stare, they never talk to me.

You look different to all the rest, well let us realise that I am not a Z!

Nor am I an X or Y, I am just me, willing to try. With perseverance, the strength of steel.

No one can ever know the journey I have faced. No one will know the level of courage it takes,

To remain positive, living the societal normal, ticking the boxes of what is acceptable.

What is normal?

I live today, after a two-year false start of what I thought it would be.

72 weeks of Chemotherapy, poked, prodded, feeling bloody.

All this including surgery, not once did I ever feel I was free,
this tumour taking over my life and invading me.

Reconfigured, redefined, oh, if only we could rewind.
Would my life be as rosy to me?

Would you take the time to get to know me and my
family?

Built on faulty foundation, my brain created an illusion.

Cruelly allowing me to continue, to move and meander
through the school run lean to.

Playing football, riding my bike, running around,
pretending to be the class clown.

Standing on my two feet with my toes in the dirt. My smile
starts to turn into a frown.

As I close my eyes, the world seems peaceful. No
judgement, no prejudice, just equal.

As my Mother whispers into my ear, time to wake up, it's
school today, I feel the fear....

What if I am never X? What if I never know Y? Will I always
be eternally seeking Z?

Will the public ever accept I?

– *Jenson*

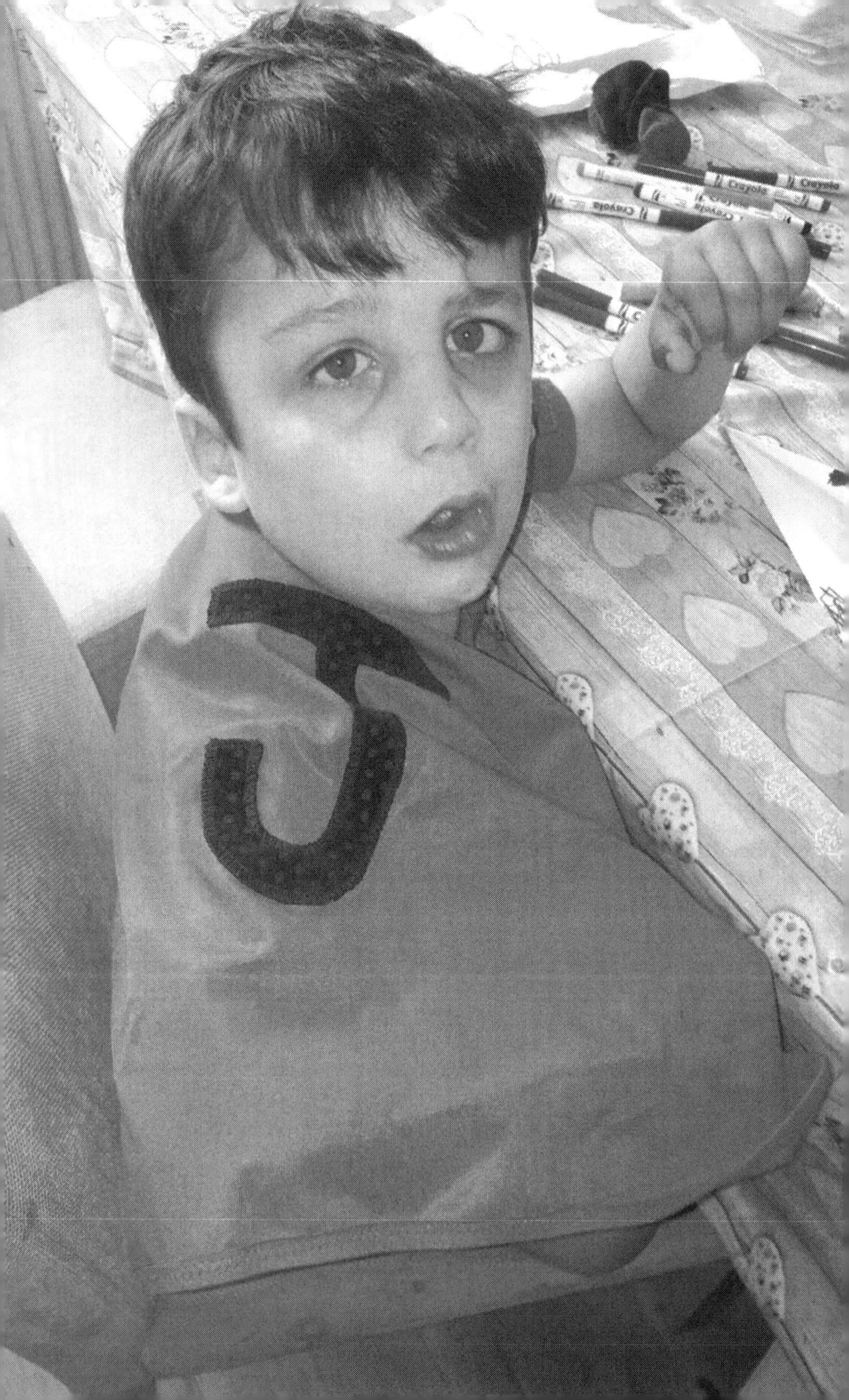
Crayola

People who get to know Jenson love him. When Jenson reaches out to others, his enthusiasm becomes infectious. The will and determination to not let his condition get the better of him earns respect and admiration from anyone who takes the time to treat or work with him.

Ah, it's Jenson

Whenever we go into the hospital now as an outpatient, the nurses always say "hello" to Jenson. They get excited when they see him, "Ah, it's Jenson."

They remember him fondly and it's purely because of the way he behaved and his courage and determination to get better. He always took in everything they said. You couldn't ask for a better student.

"Really, Jenson? Can you do this for me? Can you do that for me?", while they're trying to put in needles, tubes, so many of these tubes. He just wasn't going to be that child who screams out every two seconds because life got hard.

It was anything but that. He was tremendous. You kind of think kids are soft and they won't ever get what's going on. They're not strong enough, they won't cope, but they do. And they do so well because if that was me having a line put in, I would pass out from shock at the fact that they were trying to put it in and then they were getting it wrong. They'd take it out and put it back in again, and I was watching it all in horror. Oh my God. But Jenson's attitude was just, "Can you hurry up already? I want to watch Mr Tumble."

I couldn't believe his strength. And it wasn't once, it was every time he had a procedure, and they're very uncomfortable. He had to have this tube put in through his nose. They call it an NG tube. The nurses would have to fiddle it through and it would tickle the back of his throat. It's really uncomfortable. I was thinking, "You are going to get that in his nose? Wow. And you're going to use a rod?" But Jenson was going through it, as calm as you like.

It's like he'd put himself in this zone, "I'm not going to have anything affect me." And then it's done. Amazing. I thought, he's got these qualities that I clearly don't possess. That must be where his Dad comes in. It can't be me. It's the 50% that I didn't give him. He is awesome. He's still like it now. He's a little tough nut. If you ask him about certain things, he'll go, "Yeah, no big deal. I did this today."

He's very resilient, he's the most resilient person I know. People say, "Oh, you're so resilient." No, no, no. My son is the most resilient person I know.

Taking MRI scans in his stride

Jenson had to have an MRI, which is very difficult for a lot of people to do. When you lay in this, I call it a donut, you have to be so still. This is a boy who has global balance issues (ataxia) and can't stay still for more than a minute. He's always trying to move. I thought, this is 30 minutes of being absolute still, "How are you going to achieve that, Jenson?" I was worried for him. He wasn't worried at all. He just wanted to watch *Star Wars* through this little periscope thing they put over his head so that he could watch a film on the TV. All I could see were two great big eyes. Jenson was looking at the telly, really interested to see if his *Star Wars* DVD would play, but it didn't work.

So they had to get a different film. It turned out to be *Minions*. Thank goodness for *Minions* because he was laughing. I thought, "I can't believe it. This is such a gift." It was the best DVD out of the bunch as a backup, because at home, Jenson will watch it anytime. When they put it on, I was thinking, "Oh great. He can be still." He was fidgety a little bit at first, as he'd had no anesthetic. But he lay still. *Minions* was perfect for that scan. I just couldn't ask for anymore.

I said, "Jenson, this is awesome."

They did a scan of his head and his spine. They put the dye in Jenson's little cannula. Obviously, there is a bit of an ouchy experience with it. We don't like seeing him have that, but he just kept watching *Minions*.

I said, "All right, then Jenson. You've changed, haven't you? Go on then, put the contrast dye in."

The radiographers did it all rather quickly and it was seamlessly done. Jenson sat up and we lifted him off the scanner. Then the last action was to remove the cannula in his arm. As with all needles they can leave a tiny hole in the site of insertion. Jenson had a good vein as the blood was pouring out and needed more compression before placing a plaster on the top. As he did not have any anaesthetic, there was no need to stay any longer and we were free to go home. This was so much better than previous scans but the nerves of the results always leave you worried.

It was all over quickly, but usually it takes so much longer. So to have it done quickly, it made Jenson feel good. Then he walked out of the hospital. He used his walker, obviously, but he was very good that day. Very straight, walking controlled, and I thought, "Wow, Jenson, I can't fault you today. You got the job done."

While we were fretting and worried, I thought he was not going to be able to do it, but he surprised me. He teaches me stuff all the time. "If I can do it, Mum, you can go do it." Whatever it is.

Proving us wrong

Jenson has such a good brain, in spite of everything. He's so agile in his thinking and how he conducts himself. You can have a mature conversation with him. And he has the funniest laugh with it because he knows it can't possibly happen. I like that because it just shows the measure of his character and his nature.

If you say he can't do something, he'll prove you wrong. It's almost like pouring oil on the fire and making it more raging. It just gets him into that zone to do more. I think the way he copes is to brew up some anger and frustration to then propel himself to the next phase.

Anger and frustration can be really damaging internally, especially if you start sabotaging yourself, which I would never want Jenson to do. But he uses it in a positive way, and I do like to see him let loose. His sports are a very important way for him to channel this energy.

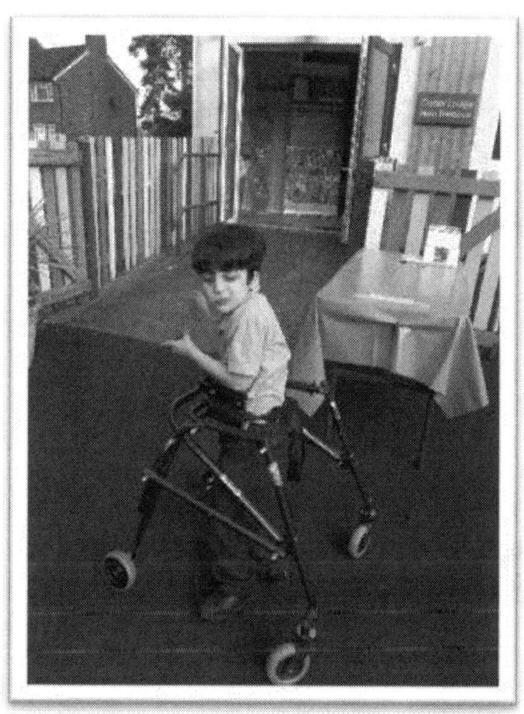

It has been amazing to watch Jenson progress. I keep pictures as I think visual diaries and archives of photos are very important to capture where something's been and where it is now. If I didn't have those photos, or videos, to show Jenson his struggle the year before, he wouldn't then appreciate where he is now. Because I know, for myself, when I'm critical of everything I do, he's also critical of himself and where he isn't at in the moment. And we have to really work hard on his confidence to ensure that he knows everything will happen in time, he just needs to give it time. So, I show him pictures of himself, and he laughs at them, and sometimes he finds it very awkward.

I said, "You just don't remember do you? Look, this is you and you couldn't say anything, and now look at you, you talk all the time. It's good, I'm not saying that you shouldn't talk, but now you talk all the time! You don't realise all the progress you're making, when you're living it every day."

He doesn't always like to be looking at videos or photos of himself struggling, but it's to give him that realisation that he's always improving. I want him to know how well he has done, because I don't think he ever realised just what he'd achieved until he saw the video, and it amazed him.

At first, he could barely get himself around using the walker. He was like a pinball and kept bashing into everything. Now, he's in control of that walker. He's using it like a toy now, he's just thinking, "Yeah, I can let myself out of it, I can sit down carefully, and I've got more stable." I think, in his mind, it's exciting, because when he's stable like that, he can do more, and then his capacity to improve continues. You can't rush it. The key thing for him, as well as me, is to learn patience. Because we both want it, but we both want it now. Everything's got to happen now. And what we've both had to learn is patience and, every now and then, Jenson would be the one telling me that, or I'd be the one telling him that, "You must wait, be patient."

Football club's mascot

The local football club loves Jenson also. They invited him to their cup game, when they were playing in the final. I ran the Bracknell half marathon that day too, so I remember it well.

Jenson was supporting me by the finish line, I could barely see him and Adam had to watch out for other people bumping into him whilst he was in his walker. As I worked my way through the finish to get my t-shirt and medal. I noticed how heavy it was. As I got through the crowds of runners I found Jenson and placed the medal round his neck. He fell forward with the weight of it.I said, "There you go, it's for you mate."

So we travelled from the race had a quick change of clothes at home then off to the football club cup final. Don't ask me how my body felt it was still fuelled with adrenaline from the marathon. Grabbing my kit bag I was on the side line ready to go on and help the players if needed. The match was close and ended up with penalties. But our team won. Hooray!!! Jenson was there holding the cup and they wanted him to be their mascot. They're inspirational. All the players had their picture taken with Jenson, and he held the cup, and it was so cool for him. He was wearing the team's kit, but it was massive, an adult-sized kit.

I said, "Come on lads, can you not find a kid's one?"

EASY as HGV
EASY HGV
FARNBOROUGH FOOT
FC ACADEMY
FARNBOROUGH
FOOTBALL CLUB
TACKLING RACISM & DISCRIMINATION

I had to try and roll his shorts up six times before they were anywhere near the size for a kid. The socks were right up to his thighs, because they were so big, and the t-shirt might as well have been a dress, but he styled it out. He looked pretty cool. It was just hilarious to see him with that cup in his hand. Then, of course, Mason wanted to take it off him. So there was a little bit of a fight between them, and we had to do a picture with Mason as well, otherwise we wouldn't get any peace.

Being of service

Jenson has been so much happier being part of a lot of communities and groups, like The Brain Tumour Charity and Sebastian's Action Trust. Sometimes, people walk past and say, "Hey, Jenson", because they've seen him somewhere, or they've seen his picture or they read something about him. They just go, "That's Jenson." Sometimes, I even wonder, "Wow, why do they say that?"

Naturally, it's because Jenson has had his say in a lot of things, with the charities and the improvements they wanted to make. His active input to the Head Smart Campaign with The Brain Tumour Charity was good, because it helped them generate something like a symptom checker that was a bit more broadly based. This means that less common symptoms that may not otherwise have been included can actually be flagged and spotted earlier by parents, so that they can get a diagnosis earlier. And they are really grateful for that.

Jenson has had a great time being of service to everybody.

Jenson's school friends

I think the friendships Jenson has at school are pretty good. He gets love letters from his girlfriends, who say they love him very much. I'm amazed, actually, that he's got so many, but it just shows how engaging he is with everybody and how well he socialises. He wants to be part of something and he can hold his own. I've seen all these qualities this year and it's blown my mind, because as a parent, you think they're going to struggle. How will he be accepted, how is everyone going to see him and receive him as a person. Are they going to be looking out for him, in his best interests.

Looking at how it has been, I reckon it has had such a positive impact on him being around others, in mainstream school. It's just really opened him up as a person. His motivation to participate inspires his school friends and their participation encourages Jenson to keep going.

Jenson and Mason – the dynamic duo

So, with all the things that were happening to his little brother when he was born, Jenson was just behaving like, "I want to be the older brother." If Mason cried, Jenson would be trying to give him toys and teddies, reassuring him with his hand, through the bars in his cot, to try and see if that would make him feel better. He was always checking on his little brother to see if he was all right.

There's not that much of an age gap between Jenson and Mason, 23 months thereabouts. It was obvious that they were either going to get on like a house on fire or they were going to absolutely hate each other, or both. That was to be expected and that's what had started to happen after Jenson's brain surgery. He could no longer be that bigger brother, the taller brother, the faster brother. He was starting all over again. Jenson had frustrations with his ability to communicate whilst Mason was talking for England. The green-eyed monster had got Jenson believing Mason was his enemy. However, through all his fights and tantrums, Jenson learnt that Mason was only trying to help. He was finding his feet too! As they both toddled around, it was a complex situation. Swimming lessons, physio sessions or just a local shopping trip became a military organised event. Time was always an issue and it was guaranteed that one of them would always want to sleep at the worst time possible. Jenson tried to regain his ability to stand, but it was too dangerous to leave him to walk in his walker alone. So, we adopted the use of a double buggy.

It was six-month-old Mason who first got a response from Jenson when he was in hospital, by annoying him with his chubby legs, flying everywhere, and hitting him. I've got a little video of this, with Mason full of joy, and Jenson looking at him with the death stare out of *Star Wars*.

He just wasn't interested in his baby brother at that moment. But gradually he started to melt, because you can't reject love like that every day. He started joining in, doing silly things. Each moment captured on my phone showed just how much Jenson loved Mason. They were just like a little Laurel and Hardy, laughing at each other. That's how their relationship has developed. They have such a good dynamic. Even now, when they're not fighting, they do have a laugh. I can hear them both laughing, especially when I'm doing something in the next room, and it's a delight.

I think that's the magic they create. They're good role models for each other. They need each other, because one way or another Mason needs Jenson's discipline and his determination to do something and to finish it, as Mason has not got any patience or focus for that long. And Jenson needs Mason's light-hearted spirit to invent creative ways of doing things.

Mason will be just singing and moving around, and going, "Hello everyone." And Jenson will be just looking at him, going "That's stupid". But then he'll become mellow too and think, well actually, it's kind of cool. Mason brings Jenson out of his shell. Social butterfly Mason has been invited to the most parties. They keep coming, these invites. I tend to break out in a sweat with all the presents, outfits and social events. We nearly always have a clash, so planning has become essential!

Then Jenson becomes like the green-eyed monster and he's easily very jealous of this, but I say, "It's not like you can't go. You're allowed to go. Siblings can go."

He says, "I don't want to go. It's a stupid party."

I go, "Are you sure about that? Because there's going to be all the things you like, music, you'll get to talk to lots of girls. It's your favorite thing, making friends? And you get to have cake."

He says, "Maybe, it's not stupid. Yeah, I might go." And then we take him anyway and he's loving it. He's in there having the best time.

That's how they work together. I think it's not going to change a whole lot. As they get older, it'll be for very different reasons in their lives that they're helping each other. You just have to watch it and admire it, because that's why I've got both of them, instead of having neither of them. There's a reason for it. And I'm very thankful for that. So I think, God, what were the possibilities at the beginning? It was too scary to think of. And Sophia gets two brothers. She does love them really, and they're going to protect her fiercely, I just know it, but she always wanted another sister. I said, don't even request that.

Sophia and Jenson

Sophia and Jenson's relationship has changed. She was heart-broken to have lost the brother she once knew and it was hard to accept. Her grief echoed within the family and made me realise that we needed to work together to move forward with our new life. This meant educating Sophia about brain tumours and how they affect Jenson. We sought the help of The Brain Tumour Charity and Sebastian's Action Trust, as we felt that she was suffering with a deep sense of loss. I would sit with her and let her have the chance to cry. By spending time together, we found comfort in learning about Jenson's condition and how brave he was to cope with it all.

His strength is something Sophia admires. I remember a point when Jenson asked where Sophia was, before he totally lost his voice. She wanted him to talk so badly after that. The bond between them is beautiful. He loves and respects her so much. Nowadays, they laugh, challenge and question everything. Sophia's Headteacher told me that she thought Sophia was one of the most resilient students she has ever met. As a parent, this was a beautiful moment to behold and one that makes me feel so grateful to still have all my children, alive, happy and healthy.

Sophia appreciates the need to have space when we face challenges with Jenson. The worries are always there, but she understands that he is recovering and that the time of his recovery may span many years. Learning to be patient but to also feel safe to know that she can enjoy playing games with Jenson has developed a deeper bond between them. Feeling isolated and not knowing when we would be back from hospital caused a lot of anxiety. We always tried to prepare as best as we could and with the use of the inhalers I made, Sophia felt closer to me when I could not be with her. The grief of losing her brother and watching him start all over again, losing her Nan and having to take extra time off school made socialising hard. Sebastian's Action Trust helped us with this. They organised events throughout the year so we could go out and, more importantly, so Sophia could go out and take some time to relax. For all those charities that have been involved, thank you. It is because of these vital resources that we are able to keep going and have a life outside of hospital.

Part VII: Resources

List of charities and support groups

Ronald McDonald House

Ronald McDonald House Charities, St.George's Hospital, Blackshaw Road, Tooting SW17 0QT, England

Website: www.rmhcuk.org.uk

Social handle: RMHCUK

Sebastian's Action Trust

Website: www.sebastiansactiontrust.org

Social media handle: SebsActionTrust on LinkedIn, Twitter, Instagram, Facebook

The Brain Tumour Charity

Website: www.thebraintumourcharity.org

Social media handle: BrainTumourOrg on LinkedIn, Twitter, Instagram, Facebook

Royal National Institute of Blind (RNIB)

Website: www.rnib.org.uk

Riding For the Disabled Association (RDA) www.rda.org.uk

Shine – the Spina Bifida, Hydrocephalus information and networking charity

Website: www.shinecharity.org.uk

Social handle: SHINEUKCharity

The Danny Green Fund

Website: www.thedannygreenfund.org.uk

Social handle: dannygreenfund

The Children's Trust Brain Injury Community Service

Website: www.thechildrenstrust.org.uk/bics

Social handle: childrens_trust

Home Start

Information on how to best support you as busy parents caring for a child with complex needs as well as younger children within your family. Offer friendship and practical help to families with children under the age of 5.

Website: www.hsbf.org.uk

The Royal Marsden

Website: www.royalmarsden.nhs.uk

Social handle: royalmarsden

Muscle Mechanics

For support and information on muscular rehabilitation

Website: www.muscle-mechanics.com

Social handle: musclemechanicsbalms or musclemechanic9

National Autistic Society

Website: www.autism.org.uk

Social handle: Autism

Motability

The Motability Scheme can help with travel and assistance equipment, or a loan vehicle. This will be custom-made to suit your needs and to provide you with more independence. The disabled person can nominate a driver if they don't drive. Cars are available to help with big equipment and wheelchair users.

Website: www.motability.org.uk

List of useful equipment for rehabilitation

Soft foam seats from Tumble Form to assist seating and gives support to the back muscles whilst eating and drinking. Can also have a tray to enable playtime and gets the kids out of bed. Suitable for children under the age of 5.

A great soft tissue massage therapist with specialism in MFR to enable communication between the brain and muscle network. Regular sessions build a stronger foundation for muscles to start to form strength. Working alongside a paediatric physio will enhance the co-ordination of movement and reduce the ataxic (shaking of the body) movements. Building muscle tone is key.

Soft face clothes and feeding bibs to protect the clothes from the excessive saliva that can be produced at mealtimes.

Tomcat Specialist Trike to give the children a chance to be outdoors and exercise safely. It is an investment for several years and can be adjusted as they get older. These trikes can also be made for adults. Check them out WWW.TOMCATUK.ORG

Orthotics to train soft muscular arches in the feet, ankle position and straighten the knees. Custom-made through your physio referral will be the best way to get this.

Snazzi Pushchair is fully supported for your child so you can travel to and from therapy sessions without injury to your back. Keeps your child safe and makes trips out exciting for them as they can engage with you and activities at table height. Check them out at www.tendercareltd.com

Muscle Mechanics Muscle balms for parents and children to help with global joint pain, muscle strain or spasms. Works with emotional mindset to lift the spirits when you are feeling overwhelmed. Check them out at www.muscle-mechanics.com

Prone Stander by Leckey enables children to learn how to regulate the pressures behind their eyes and to hold themselves in a standing position. Comes with additional tools to help them paint, draw, play with therapy toys. Usually prescribed by the physio team and can be funded through your hospital therapy team or organisation. Some pieces can be loaned and then returned. Check them out at www.leckey.com

Toilet frames and seating to help them become more independent. We actually sourced this through a company based in England called The Complete Care Shop. They have a great selection of care equipment for kids. It is always best to chat with the occupational therapist first before adding anything, as they can get equipment for you. But you can check them out at www.disableliving.co.uk/online-shop/

DMO orthotic suits. Brilliant at sensory feedback to the brain through the use of compression. This has helped Jenson enormously. He wears it like it is his superhero suit. All the muscles feel secure but also learn to move with the additional restriction that we would naturally provide, but in this case, Jenson had lost this instinctive skill to do this and needed to relearn how to move and adjust balance where necessary. This continues to be an issue but has improved significantly with this piece of kit. Check them out at www.dmorthotics.com

Nimbo Posture Walker for all outdoor activities when children are able to hold themselves up and move with confidence. It is usually best to get this when they have mastered the art of 'bear walking' or crawling securely. Has a variety of tools to add to the frame and keep your child safe. Jenson loves his walker and now uses it to beat me to the car at the school run! Check them out at www.inspiredbydrive.com

Supine Stander. Helps to elevate the person and get used to being vertical after brain surgery, this is something that requires frequent use to be able to reinforce a better regulation of gravity and blood flow as well as the pressure experienced behind the eyes. We sourced this through the hospital and used it over the Christmas period before going to The Children's Trust. Check them out at www.jiraffe.org.uk

Etac R82. An essential walking aid that can be adjusted with you. I love this piece of equipment and it has served Jenson well over the last few years. The physio team agreed it would give much more independence at school if Jenson could get around by himself and reduce the health and safety concerns around us as parents and his one-to-one specialist. Check them out at www.R82.co.uk

Talk Tools Therapists. These are a range of speech and language tools to use with your child when they are learning to use their mouth to create the right shape to formulate the correct word sounds. Bite blocks, whistles, chew toys, blowing bubbles and sustainable straws to encourage the correct placement of lips to drink from a cup. It is incredible what these Talk Tools therapists can achieve with your children. Always ask what they can suggest first then build up your tools. Meal times can be dealt with using a choice of at least 10 different spoons and plate guards, Dycem grip matting and weighted cutlery. Feeding will be a challenge. Check them out at http://www.eg-training.co.uk

Seating systems to help with everyday activities such as eating, drinking, reading and writing. In the beginning, it will be very supportive and will be prescribed by physios to help until certain muscle strengths have been achieved. Then you can move onto another system without all the straps and pelvic supports. Seating needs to be good to enable better posture and to free the hands to create, write or play. Kids can spend so much time trying to hold themselves in the right position that it becomes exhausting for them.

Technical medical terms explained

Pilocytic Astrocytoma: This is an accumulation of rogue astrocytes that form an eventual solid mass (tumour). Astrocytes are the most abundant cells in the brain. They provide support and protection to the neurons and they help to pass messages between the neurons. They are vital to processing information in the brain. There are grades 1-4, with 4 being the most deadly and difficult tumour to treat. Low grade would be classed as 1, with the biopsy indicating a benign tumour (non-cancerous). Pilocyctic is a term for 'hair like cells', which are slow growing and generally contained within one area.

Cerebral Spinal Fluid (CSF): This is a clear fluid that flows through the ventricles and over the surface of the spinal cord and brain, where it is absorbed. Provides an element of protection and helps to supply the brain with vitamins, may also help removes any toxins.

Endoscopic Third Ventriculostomy (ETV): Is a procedure used to treat hydrocephalus as an alternative to a shunt. Helps to redirect the flow of brain fluid to reduce the pressure experienced in the brain. Headaches can be a sign that this pressure in the brain is too high. A hole is created in the third ventricle which allows the fluid into the area that lines the brain and spinal cord called the Sub Arachnoid Space. Once the fluid is there, it can be absorbed.

External Ventricular Drain (EVD): This is an external catheter used to drain excess CSF from the brain into a measurable glass drain, which can later be released into a bag to be collected. This is usually put in place when there is an infection. Jenson had severe brain infection and required an urgent procedure to relieve the brain of this fluid but to also treat it. This EVD helped the surgeons to observe how Jenson was responding to treatment. Once it was clear in appearance, they could then operate and install an internal shunt to regulate the brain pressures.

Hydrocephalus: Occurs when the production of cerebro-spinal fluid flowing around the brain and spinal cord is greater than the absorption. If the drainage pathways are obstructed (i.e. with a brain tumour), the fluid accumulates in the cerebral ventricles leading to raised intracranial pressure. So in other words a compression of the brain tissue.

Shunt: A shunt is a way to control increased pressure inside the head caused by hydrocephalus. They are thin tubes that help redirect the cerebral spinal fluid to a place where it can be absorbed.

Ventriculo-peritoneal Shunt (VP Shunt): This is positioned with the head of the catheter placed within the ventricles 3-4. The end of the catheter finishes in the space surrounding the intestines (the peritoneum). Fluid here is similar to CSF. So the CSF mixes with this fluid and gets absorbed. If the shunt has a blockage and becomes infected, the membrane covering the intestines can block the end of the shunt. Pressure can be adjusted to suit the individual. Sometimes this can be programmable, it depends on each case. Fixed pressure is another option, which Jenson has in place.

Posterior fossa syndrome: This is a syndrome that has been reported to occur within thirty percent of children that undergo surgery to the back of the brain. The severity of the condition varies considerably from one child to the next. Causes of this syndrome are still unclear but it occurs when operations on the cerebellum and brain stem disrupt the communication from the back of the brain to the front. Some research suggests that it is the interruption of a pathway in the brain that sends signals from the cerebellum to parts of the brain that process information, sensations and body movements. Essentially, all muscle movements must be relearnt to enable a new neural pathway to be formed to communicate instructions and process information. This can take many years and the symptoms may be lifelong.

Nasal gastric tube or NG tube for short. Is a thin flexible plastic tube that gets inserted into the nose all the way down to the stomach. This allows special liquid feed formula and medication to be administered when the person is unable to swallow safely or the muscles within the body are too weak to process food naturally.

What is an aspirate?

When children have a nasal gastric tube inserted, it usually has to pass up through the nose and down the oesophagus towards the stomach. When the position is correct, you can then take a syringe and attach it to the connector on the outside and test for an aspirate. An aspirate is a way of acknowledging the tube is in the right place and that the formula feeds are being processed in the stomach. Sometimes Jenson could not digest his food and this led to the whole feed being syringed out of his stomach. The position of the tube was very important as this was the channel the nurses would use to administer medication and pain relief. They were not the most comfortable to insert and Jenson needed a loving cuddle to relax him enough to enable the tube to go up through his nose. He said it used to tickle the back of his throat. Every mealtime, we would have to test for an aspirate to ensure that the tube hadn't moved, before he could have his formula feed. Occasionally, it would need adjusting or Jenson would need to change his sitting position to move the tube to get an aspirate.

Physiotherapy: Paediatric physiotherapists work with all the movements and muscle functionality. They are involved with co-ordination, balance and cardiovascular muscle recovery. The education of the children on how to move and how to practise to improve their mobility is invaluable.

Occupational Therapy: This helps children and adults to learn how to take care of themselves as well as participating in everyday life activities. This would include dressing, washing themselves, eating, play and leisure time hobbies, and adapting to school life using writing equipment and hand exercises to hold pencils and pens, even cutlery, the best way possible.

Speech and Language Therapy (SALT): Focuses on the formation of words and how the children communicate using their physical mobility of the jaw, chin and lips. This can be during conversation with regards to processing information or through eating and chewing food. They help to identify any swallowing issues or sensitivities to food.

Ophthalmologists: Are specialist eye and vision doctors. Those that have experience in posterior fossa syndrome are the best to consult with regards to ability and field of vision. They understand that the recovery process is fluid and that the children are likely to keep improving with time.

Orthotists: Are specialist creators of medical supports for patients. These can range from foot issues to global ataxia, which requires assistance to control on a daily basis until recovery.

Dietitian: Is an expert in treating types of malnutrition and applying medical nutrition therapy to aid in recovery or to sustain a healthy body. They will calculate and advise what would be best for the patient with regards to their General Condition Status.

Clinical Nurse Specialist (CNS): Is an advanced practice registered nurse. They provide direct care to patients within a specialty like paediatric oncology.

Oncologists: Specialist doctors that help direct the best medical pathway for a variety of cancers. They organise and execute nuclear medicine with the objective to reduce symptoms experienced and prolong the life expectancy of the patient.

Bibliography

Balaster, Cavin (2017). How to Feed a Brain. Nutrition for Optimal Brain Function and Repair. Austin, TX.

Beattie, Melody (1992). Codependent No More. How to Stop Controlling Others and Start Caring for Yourself. Minnesota, Hazelden Publishing.

Bruce, Debra Fulghum, PhD (2022, August 28) Grief and Depression. WebMD. Retrieved from https://www.webmd.com/depression/guide/depression-grief

Children's Cancer and Leukaemia Group (2017,November 26). Posterior fossa syndrome. Information for parents of a child with PFS.

Dispenza, Joe, Dr (2014). You Are The Placebo, Making Your Mind Matter. United States, CA: Haye House Publishing.

Great Ormond Street Hospital (2022, November 10). Cited https://www.gosh.nhs.uk/teenagers/tests-and-treatments/nasogastric-ng-tube-feeding/

Keown M.B. Ch.B. Lic. Ac, Daniel, Dr (2014). The Spark in the Machine, How the Science of Acupuncture Explains the Mysteries of Western Medicine. London. Singing Dragon.

The Children's Trust (2022, November 15). Brain Injury Community Service. Effects of acquired brain injury. Tadworth, Surrey.

The Brain Tumour Charity (2017, November 12). Hill, Peter, PhD. The Brain Tumour Charity, London, UK. Astrocytoma, your notes. Saving lives through research, information, awareness & policy.

Shine (2018, May 21). Your Child and Hydrocephalus. For families of children with hydrocephalus and the professionals working with them. Additional information. Peterborough, UK. Pages 77-81

St George's Hospital, NHS Trust. Paediatric Neurosciences (2012, September 10). Parent and patient information, Hydrocephalus and treatment. Endoscopic Third Ventriculostomy (ETV) London, UK.

About the Author

Kimberley Shamtally is an Entrepreneur, Physical Therapist and Best-Selling Author. She is a mother to three children and an advocate for children who have lost their voice within society. With experience of Autism Spectrum Disorders, Kimberley has developed a way of communicating with children using sensory education. Identifying her own anxiety and learning ways to live with it, she realised that she could overcome adversity, so that she could become the best version of herself. Now these skills and therapies can help many parents and adults that find dealing with life-changing events overwhelming.

The indescribable pain experienced as a parent had a profound effect on how Kimberley began to live her life. It was a place of darkness at times with no end in sight. It does not matter how low you feel, you must find a way to carry on. Her children relied on her, and her family needed stability.

Through the tragedy of her son's brain tumour diagnosis and the Covid lockdown, Kimberley invented a series of therapeutic balm kits. She had to change direction due to the physical aromatherapy business she'd spent 10 years building having to close. It took perseverance and tenacity. But the new business also created an opportunity for her to help others rather than stay overwhelmed with fear, living with perpetual life changing situations. The knowledge and wisdom of retraining her son's movements have now been used to help many adults achieve better physical health after injury.

During her son's illness, as a mother to three children, she could see that she was not taking care of herself properly. Her weight had increased significantly due to living from day to day rather than looking at the long-term effects of unhealthy living. She started running as a way of coping with stress and improving her mental health, but it served another purpose. By running, she reduced her weight and helped her physical body to heal from the trauma that she had been faced with. She has now run over two hundred miles for charity, raising awareness of her son's condition, as well as vital funds for Sebastian's Action Trust. This charity became a lifeline for her family whilst living in isolation during the pandemic, as her son continued his chemotherapy treatment.

She completed the Virtual London Marathon in 2021 after the heart break of losing her mother. Learning to let go of someone she loved was the hardest thing she could do but also the kindest. Yet, to have to do that twice, a change of perspective was overdue. With a new lease of life, Kimberley launched the Muscle Mechanics online shop, providing natural therapeutic remedies to aid healing of the mind and body. Her client base started to build again, and the love of helping others through healing and physical therapies became cathartic. Sometimes life can be one long painful experience or a series of trials. Through grief, Kimberley created a series of balms to ease those moments, so she could go on and rebuild those dreams she still felt in her heart.

Muscle Mechanics

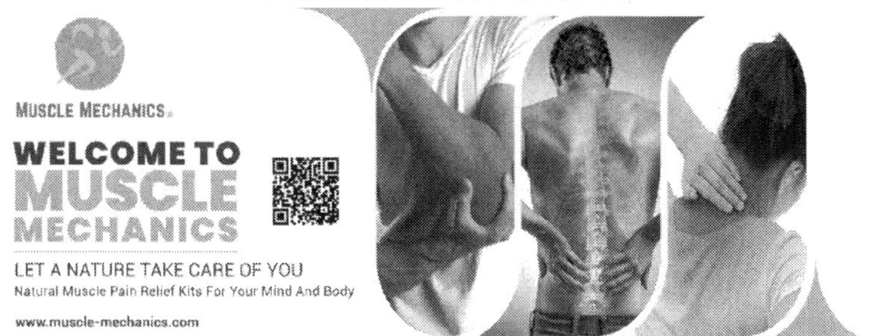

My business, Muscle Mechanics Balms, helps people find that inner peace during chaotic times, of recovery from a sporting injury or the sadness of grief. Each client can present as healthy, but they may have a reoccurring pain that never seems to go away. If this affects them physically, I enjoy investigating the root cause of this to establish a better way of moving so they can go on and enjoy the sport they love or a favourite hobby. Showing that clients can find another way to deal with pain helps them to move forward and change their lives to become more in tune with themselves then the outside world. With so many options and opinions of how we should live our lives, I take a different approach and ask them what do they want? What would make the biggest impact if they could move better? Then I listen and wait. This can take clients a while to understand that I am not here to enforce a way of living but to understand them. Giving them the chance to be listened to, is immensely powerful and sometimes tears will fall but this is all part of clearing the suppressed feelings we can all hold inside.

My inspiration to be the best person I can be comes from my children. When I see those faces every morning and before they go to bed, I am incredibly grateful to have them in my life. I remember at one point both of my boys' lives were in danger and imagining a life without them, I just simply could not comprehend that. Without sounding like a cliché, every facet of my personality is under evaluation and assessed to the maximum with their needs and especially my son Jenson's rehabilitation needs. If I did not have a clue about something, I made it my mission to find out all that I could. I listen to Tony Robbins and find his approach to working through the yukky stuff in life works for me. Sometimes you need to face those areas head on and break each problem down by visualising a solution. Allowing that creativity to flow. David Goggin's incredible way of optimising his body through the hardest physical challenges he can find, inspires me to keep going and to not get comfortable when you know deep down you want to do more but find excuses not to. Making the impossible, possible is a saying we love in our house.

Inspired, by the beauty of the human body. How one system relies on another and the harmony that occurs to keep us in the right rhythm with the activity we are involved in. When we run and it becomes effortless, each muscle, tendon and ligament form a perfect relationship to release that raw speed and power. The endurance that our skin takes when we prepare for motherhood. How we evolve as we train to become an athlete of our own life. Seeing food as our medicine to fuel for the day, clearing all that brain fog that comes with the relentless stress of our environment that we live in. Acknowledging a series of patterns that facilitate movement and how we programme ourselves on an individual basis, we can affect change anytime we want. This is the best part of my work, showing individuals that they can achieve what they desire so long as they know what it is that they want. Science and medicine are interests of mine and I like to read latest research and innovations projects to help my clients achieve a better outcome.

This year Muscle Mechanics has achieved a special recognition from The Federation of Holistic Therapists. This felt like we had finally arrived as a service that is valued for the volunteering and challenging work that goes into educating others about alternative therapies. We came runner up at The Business Success Recognition Awards within the Overcoming Adversity category. As a full time carer to my son that continues to recover from a brain tumour diagnosis in 2017, this nomination gave me the chance to show that carers can have financial turmoil and restriction to how they earn but with the right team around them they can go on to build sustainable businesses that give their loved ones the support they need. Sometimes we must generate a new pathway to succeed and through the toughest challenges we show of what we are capable. The biggest breakthrough, achieving an editorial within Men's Health Magazine. We wanted to build seriously as a family business and with all our research into how our blends work and the sporting events that we had attended. This was a giant step in the right direction. My son's use of all the balm products demonstrates how gentle and versatile the blend can be. He had a series of major operations and life saving medical treatment, he was the right case study for this to become a go to method of treating everyday aches and pains. Personally, I have achieved my running goals of completing a virtual London Marathon and seven half marathons using my blends within the recovery period. Assisting many more marathon runners at the national shows. Our aim is to help as many people as we can, to feel better.

The creation of these balms started in my kitchen with the children during lockdown. Entertaining the three or them by learning to bake, my invention needed the right time to set. As they were carefully decanted into dessert pots, the timer went off for the cakes. Covered in icing sugar, Jenson replies. " The jelly has set Mummy," The balm had definitely set and it felt smooth and more importantly it worked on my sore back!

Visit my website for more information:

www.muscle-mechanics.com

Or visit my linktr.ee/kshamtally

2022
OFFICIAL HONOREE
BRAINZ 500 GLOBAL
CAROLINE WINKVIST
FREDRIK ELFQVIST

★★★★★
BRAINZ
500
GLOBAL

27.05.22

To: Business Success Recognition Awards Panel

It is my absolute pleasure to provide **Kim Shamtally** with a testimonial.

I am blessed to be a leader in a global media organisation (NBCUniversal) and meet with business professionals around the world. I met Kim on a personal level though to support me overcome a sporting injury several years ago and have been a client ever since because Kim is both amazing and gifted at what she does but also truly cares about her clients.

Kim is simply an incredible human being. You cannot overstate how challenging the personal circumstances Kim has had to face with her son Jenson's condition who she came close to losing several times but fought and continues to fight for him at every step while at the same time dealing with close family loss. Throughout all this Kim has held her head high, shown incredible resilience and strength and focussed her energy on supporting and raising awareness and money for others dealing with similar considers to Jenson all while continuing to grow Muscle Mechanics with the goal of heeling and bringing others back to full physical and mental health at a time when they need it the most.

Many people would have frankly given up long ago. Kim is relentless in overcoming adversity and moreover she does this with such a positive attitude. Inspiration is a word that is thrown around a lot, but Kim is truly inspirational! I wish Muscle Mechanics continued success and that Jenson's Journey will have the lasting impact in supporting other families Kim hopes it will. If I could, I would vote 1000 times over for Kim for this award.

Best regards
Russell

Kimberley Shamtally, Jenson's Journey to Recovery

27.05.22

To: Business Success Recognition Awards Panel

It is my absolute pleasure to provide Kim Shamtally with a testimonial

I am blessed to be a leader in a global media organisation (NBCUniversal) and meet with business professionals around the world. I met Kim on a personal level though to support me overcome a sporting injury several years ago and have been a client ever since because Kim is both amazing and gifted at what she does but also truly cares about her clients.

Kim is simply an incredible human being. You cannot overstate how challenging the personal circumstances Kim has had to face with her son Jenson's condition who she came close to losing several times but fought and continues to fight for him at every step while at the same time dealing with close family loss. Throughout all this Kim has held her head high, shown incredible resilience and strength and focussed her energy on supporting and raising awareness and money for others dealing with similar considers to Jenson all while continuing to grow Muscle Mechanics with the goal of heeling and bringing others back to full physical and mental health at a time when they need it the most.

Many people would have frankly given up long ago. Kim is relentless in overcoming adversity and moreover she does this with such a positive attitude. Inspiration is a word that is thrown around a lot, but Kim is truly inspirational! I wish Muscle Mechanics continued success and that Jenson's Journey will have the lasting impact in supporting other families Kim hopes it will. If I could, I would vote 1000 times over for Kim for this award.

Best regards
Russell

Here for families of
seriously-ill children. Always.

Kim Shamtally

31st January 2022

Dear Kim,

The past two years have been incredibly difficult for everyone; especially for you and your family having endured so much uncertainty and isolation which continues to be with us. Despite this, you have found the time and motivation to help the Trust get through this period. We could not have done this without the generosity and commitment of you – our amazing supporter.

To acknowledge the wonderful support you have kindly given us throughout this difficult time, I have the pleasure in inviting you to one of the receptions we are hosting to thank you and everyone who has been here for us and our families over the past two years. The receptions will be held at The Bluebells in Hampshire on Wednesday 9th March 2022, and at The Woodlands in Berkshire on Wednesday 23rd March 2022.

Further details of the receptions are provided on the invitation enclosed with this letter. I do hope you will be able to join us at one of these events.

Our sincere thanks and appreciation go to all who helped to make Sebastian's Action Trust an innovative, responsive and connected 'family of families', and I look forward to welcoming you to one of the forthcoming celebrations.

Yours sincerely,

Jane Gates

Jane Gates OBE
Chief Executive Officer
Sebastian's Action Trust
01344 622500 / 07879 999677 jane@sebastiansactiontrust.org

Sebastian's Action Trust
The Woodlands, Upper Broadmoor Road, Crowthorne, Berkshire RG45 7FN
Tel: 01344 622500 info@sebastiansactiontrust.org www.sebastiansactiontrust.org

If you no longer wish to receive letters or emails from Sebastian's Action Trust please email info@sebastiansactiontrust.org

 /SebsActionTrust  /SebsActionTrust

 /SebsActionTrust  /SebsActionTrust

together Lives

Sebastian's Action Trust

Dear Kim

The past two years have been incredibly difficult for everyone; especially for you and your family having endured so much uncertainty and isolation which continues to be with us. Despite this, you have found the time and motivation to help the Trust get through this period. We could not have done this without the generosity and commitment of you - our amazing supporter.

To acknowledge the wonderful support you have kindly given us throughout this difficult time, I have the pleasure in inviting you to one of the receptions we are hosting to thank you and everyone who has been here for us and our families over the past two years. The receptions will be held at The Bluebells in Hampshire on Wednesday 9 March 2022 and at The Woodlands in Berkshire on Wednesday 23 March 2022.

Further details of the receptions are provided on the invitation enclosed with this letter. I do hope you will be able to join us at one of these events.

Keep moving towards the finish line with Muscle Mechanics Balm

Professionally blended Muscle Mechanics balms, with essential oils, are kind to your skin and help you relax muscles that are tired from exercise or working long hours. The balms are enriched with shea butter to moisturise so they sink into the skin, helping you to massage tight muscles and leaving you feeling relaxed and invigorated. With over 15 years' experience in aromatherapy, Muscle Mechanics is a family business that uses natural ways to manage everyday physical challenges. Made in the UK, the balms come in tins to travel with you wherever you need.

• Lasting up to four hours after application, a little goes a long way. So order your Muscle Mechanics balm kit today at muscle-mechanics.com, or call [illegible]

The latest technologies to treat atrial fibrillation

Atrial fibrillation (AF) is one of the leading causes of stroke, and significant symptoms include shortness of breath, tiredness and palpitations arising from irregular heartbeats. The rapid pace of scientific and technological advancement has enabled ever more safer and effective treatments for people with this troublesome and serious condition.

Dr Malcolm Finlay has emerged as a recognised clinician and innovator in this fast-moving area, particularly known for his expertise in treatments for AF. He specialises in using a state-of-the-art heart minimally invasive surgery called 'catheter ablation' to treat atrial fibrillation, as well as in pacemaker technologies. The common thread across his work is to use novel approaches to improve patient treatments. Qualifying from the University of Oxford, he read his PhD at University College London and was appointed as consultant cardiologist at St Bartholomew's Hospital in 2014. He's also an honorary clinical reader at Queen Mary University of London.

"The improvements in technology now allow day-case ablation treatment to be performed", he says. "We've been able to move from requiring two nights in hospital to

Printed in Great Britain
by Amazon

20937866R00140